The ABCs of the ADA

Funded by

MISSION COLLEGE

Carl D. Perkins Vocational and Technical Education Act Grant

The ABCs of the ADA

*Your Early Childhood Program's Guide
to the Americans with Disabilities Act*

by

Karren Ikeda Wood, Ed.D., OTR

and

Victoria Youcha, Ed.D.

·P A U L·H·
BROOKES
PUBLISHING C^{O.}®

Baltimore • London • Sydney

Paul H. Brookes Publishing Co.
Post Office Box 10624
Baltimore, Maryland 21285-0624
www.brookespublishing.com

Typeset by Integrated Publishing Solutions, Grand Rapids, Michigan.
Manufactured in the United States of America by
Versa Press, Inc., East Peoria, Illinois.

The information provided in this book is in no way meant to substitute for legal advice.
This book is sold without warranties of any kind, express or implied, and the publisher
and authors disclaim any liability, loss, or damage caused by the contents of this book.

The individuals described in this book are composites or real people whose situations
have been masked and are based on the authors' experiences. Names and identifying
details have been changed to protect confidentiality.

The photograph that appears on the cover is used by permission of the individual
pictured and his parents.

Library of Congress Cataloging-in-Publication Data
Wood, Karren Ikeda.
The ABCs of the ADA: Your early childhood program's guide to the Americans with
Disabilities Act/ by Karren Wood and Victoria Youcha [2nd ed.].
    p.   cm.
Updated ed. of: Child care and the ADA: A handbook for inclusive programs / Victoria
Youcha Rab and Karren Ikeda Wood with a special contribution from Janeen Taylor. 1995.
Includes bibliographical references and index.
ISBN-13: 978-1-55766-933-9
ISBN-10: 1-55766-933-3
1.   Day care centers—Law and legislation—United States.   2.   Child care services—Law
and legislation—United States.   3.   Early childhood education—Law and legislation—
United States.   4.   Children with disabilities—Legal status, laws, etc.—United States.
5.   Discrimination against people with disabilities—Law and legislation—United States.
6.   United States. Americans with Disabilities Act of 1990.   I.   Rab, Victoria Youcha.
II.   Rab, Victoria Youcha. Child care and the ADA.   III.   Title.

KF2042.D3R33 2009
344.7303'2712—dc22   2008036057

British Library Cataloguing in Publication data are available from the British Library.

2012   2011   2010   2009   2008

10   9   8   7   6   5   4   3   2   1

Contents

Appendixes

About the Authors

Karren Ikeda Wood, Ed.D., OTR, is currently a private educational consultant. Her formal education was in special education and occupational therapy. Her initial work experience in occupational therapy gave her a solid grounding in pediatric assessment and child development. She has provided services to preschool children in public and private programs for children with disabilities and has also provided these services in community-based settings. She assisted the Arizona Early Intervention Program in developing and providing standards of practice training for early intervention providers. Her most recent work experiences include supporting the efforts of community-based child care programs to create library areas focusing on literacy activities and mentoring emergent leaders in the field of early care and education.

Victoria Youcha, Ed.D., is currently Director of BrainLine, a national multimedia project on traumatic brain injury at WETA, the public television station serving greater Washington, D.C. She was the founding director of the Court Teams for Maltreated Infants and Toddlers Project at ZERO TO THREE: National Center for Infants, Toddlers and Families. Prior to joining ZERO TO THREE, she taught at The George Washington University and directed the early childhood special education master's degree program at the Alexandria Graduate Education Center. Dr. Youcha has worked with young children and their families for more than 30 years in a variety of roles, including directing an early intervention program, working as a child development specialist, and supporting early childhood programs to include children with disabilities. She has authored a variety of publications related to abuse and neglect, inclusion, and disabilities.

Foreword to the Second Edition

Early childhood development is gaining attention in the United States and around the world. States are investing more and more resources during the early years, and programs are growing for preschoolers and for children under 3. Yet, for far too many children and for far too long, the door to such opportunities has been hard to open, particularly for children with special needs—children with other abilities and potential. This book by Karren Ikeda Wood and Victoria Youcha hopes to make the opening of those doors much easier by helping to provide access, support, and quality early childhood experiences to all children and their families.

I have been fortunate over the past 30 years to travel the country working with others on behalf of young children. During those years, especially in the mid-1990s when serving as the Associate Commissioner of the Child Care Bureau and later at Deputy Assistant Secretary for Children and Families in the U.S. Department of Health and Human Services, I often met parents of children with disabilities who struggled to find and maintain quality services for their young children. While the abilities of their children and their own life circumstances often varied, their stories were too often the same—there were few options for their children, few people trained and sensitive to their special circumstances, and too few supports for them as they navigated their way through the system.

This is a straightforward book and an important resource for program administrators, teachers, child care providers, parents, and all of those who believe in giving equal opportunities to all children. It is for those who advocate to ensure that our youngest children with special needs have full access to every opportunity possible, for those who want to ensure that there is full integration of children with diverse abilities into our programs, and for those who want to provide the very best services to families. It is the type of book that should be on the desk of every early childhood program administrator, read and referred to as they move to implement a successful program that is welcoming to all children and staff who may bring a range of abilities and backgrounds.

The opening chapters provide the policy background on the Americans with Disabilities Act (ADA) of 1990 (PL 101-336), the landmark legislation that worked to ensure the civil rights of millions of Americans with disabilities and moved to eliminate the history of discrimination, including the discrimination against the full inclusion of children into early childhood programs. Along with specific details about the ADA, the opening chapters guide those of us in the children's community less familiar with the specifics of the ADA through the various provisions of this law, along with other disability laws that affect the presence of children in early childhood programs.

This basic information is followed by critically important chapters that should help program administrators and others review their programs and ensure compliance with the provisions of the law. Once familiar with the law, a thorough program review can begin to transform services to become more responsive, more inclusive, and more diverse. Understanding the core components of a high-quality program is essential. The review includes not only the accommodations in the physical facility but also an important emphasis on staff development, planning, and implementation.

Once this review is completed, it is the everyday work around communication with staff and families that is the heart of making the ADA work for children. The book addresses the normal fears that come when people face unfamiliar circumstances and experience the need to change. The conversation starters included in some of the chapters bring the potential of the law to life and remind all of us about the importance of supportive, well-informed, and passionate staff to the important work of caring for children and appreciating diversity.

All parents need to feel that their children are special. Early childhood programs can help foster this feeling by bringing parents and children together, promoting attachment and bonding, and making parents feel proud of every accomplishment. It is the competent and supportive teacher or program director who can make all the difference in the daily lives of children and families. It is the effective program that can help build parental confidence and set children on a journey for lifelong learning regardless of their different abilities.

Reading through this book made me reflect back to my early days working in Head Start, where I learned firsthand the benefits of inclusion to both the child with a disability and to the children and adults who learned from the child with a disability. I remember the smile on a mother's face when she entered the room and saw her child with limited vision playing in the block corner with other children; the special relationship that grew between a senior volunteer and a little boy who had delayed speech; or the empathy and compassion that grew as children looked after one another, pushing wheelchairs, asking for turns, seeing just another playmate or a special friend where adults might have seen special needs.

I hope that the important provisions of the ADA and the potential that it, along with other related legislation, has for transforming the lives of children and supporting their families will inspire others. Only when we all take action to fulfill this potential will the law come alive, and the joy of learning that is the heart and soul of a good early childhood program will be open to all young children across the country and around the world.

Joan Lombardi, Ph.D.
Washington, D.C.

Reference

Americans with Disabilities Act of 1990, PL 101-336, 42 U.S.C. §§ 12101 *et seq.*

Preface to the Second Edition

Eighteen years have passed since the Americans with Disabilities Act (ADA) of 1990 (PL 101-336) became law, and 13 years have passed since the publication of the previous edition of this book, *Child Care and the ADA: A Handbook for Inclusive Programs* (Rab & Wood, 1995). As this book goes to press, the *Federal Register* has released proposed rule making. Although there has been progress, children with disabilities are still denied access to many community programs. Too many early childhood programs still do not routinely serve children with special needs. We strongly believe that children with disabilities should have the opportunity to participate in regular early childhood programs with their friends.

This book is for administrators of center-based, early childhood programs to help them understand and comply with the law and, even more importantly, to promote high-quality settings where children with and without disabilities can learn together. There are well-documented benefits of serving children with and without disabilities in the same setting. The focus of this book is on implementing strategies that support successful inclusion. Strong leadership is critical to providing the support that teachers, families, and children need to make inclusion work.

All children deserve high-quality early learning experiences, and we hope that this book will assist administrators providing such programs. The ADA challenges all of us to continue to develop strategies that support developmentally appropriate, quality programs for all children.

References

Americans with Disabilities Act of 1990, PL 101-336, 42 U.S.C §§ 12101 *et seq.*

Rab, V.Y., & Wood, K.I. (1995). *Child care and the ADA: A handbook for inclusive programs.* Baltimore: Paul H. Brookes Publishing Co.

Acknowledgments

Many thanks to the professional community, who have continued to ask us hard questions and seek answers about how best to support the development of all young children. We would like to acknowledge the patience and professionalism of our Paul H. Brookes Publishing Co. editors, Marie Abate and Astrid Pohl Zuckerman. Thanks to our families who supported us and gave up time for this endeavor.

*To the many early childhood professionals, children,
and families who have shared their experiences with us
and who have continued to advocate for programs of
high quality that meet the needs of all children*

—Karren Ikeda Wood

For Leon

—Victoria Youcha

Introduction

When parents join the workforce, they face a difficult decision. They must make choices about who will care for their children, how their children will be cared for, and where their children will be cared for. These are difficult questions that involve additional considerations, such as cost and transportation. The public is also becoming more educated about early brain development and the need for quality in early childhood programs. Evidence is accumulating about who is attending early childhood programs and the importance of early experiences.

The demand for quality early childhood programs has continued to grow during the past 2 decades (Annie E. Casey Foundation, 1998; Children's Defense Fund, 1998). In 1988, 26% of the children younger than 5 years with working mothers were in center-based care. The current estimate of children under the age of 5 in some type of child care arrangement is close to 63% (Mulligan, Brimhall, & West, 2005; National Association of Child Care Resource and Referral Agencies [NACCRRA], 2006). Of these children, 3 out of 10 are in center-based care (Urban Institute, 2004).

Several factors have contributed to the high demand for quality early childhood programs. First, the changing demographics of the work force have fueled the increased demand. The most recently reported number of families with two working parents with children under the age of 6 was 55.6%. In single-parent households, 83.8% of men and 64.7% of women with children under 6 years of age were working (Bureau of Labor Statistics, 2006).

Parents of children with disabilities are part of this trend. In data collected in 2005, the U.S. Department of Education, Office of Special Education Programs, reported that approximately 50% of the nearly 500,000 identified children with disabilities were being served in early childhood programs with their nondisabled peers. This means that parents of children with disabilities are looking for inclusive early childhood programs.

As values and beliefs about appropriate programming for children with disabilities have changed, an evolution in philosophy about more inclusive group settings for children with disabilities has taken place (Child Care Plus, 2007). Although child care and special education in segregated settings still exist (U.S. Department of Education, 2005), the demand for and participation in less segregated options is growing. Parents of children with disabilities are seeking community-based early childhood programs that will make accommodations for their children. Discrimination still limits the availability of such programs. Despite the legislative mandate of the Americans with Disabilities Act (ADA) of 1990 (PL 101-336), prejudice and barriers to accessibility prevent children with disabilities from being admitted to early childhood programs.

Affordability

Not only has the demand for early education programs risen, but the costs have also increased. In 2008, the annual fee for full-time, center-based infant care ranges from $4,020 to $14,225. For a child of 4, the center-based fees range from $3,900 to $10,200 per year. Those figures are striking compared to the average cost of a year of public higher education at $5,132. For a family below the poverty level, 25% of their average income will be spent on child care (NACCRRA, 2006).

Importance of Early Learning Environments

The recent research and findings about the brain and its impact on early development makes quality early education a priority to many people (Shonkoff & Phillips, 2000). States are now considering making public early childhood programs available in existing school systems (Pre[K]now, 2007) and increasing the length of the day for kindergarteners.

Early childhood programs have moved beyond their role of primarily providing opportunities for socialization and parent respite. Research on development of the young child and the importance of early brain development has shifted more to providing quality experiences in relationships with other children and adults and real learning opportunities. Carefully planned learning environments and well-trained, supportive adults are key to the successful future development of all children.

Using This Book

Children with and without disabilities can and should have the chance to play, learn, and grow together. The ADA provides the legal basis for this equal access, and solid research confirms its benefit to all children.

This book provides early childhood program administrators with basic information about the ADA and how to comply with its requirements. The first three chapters introduce administrators to other disability legislation that can support quality inclusive efforts and provides guidance on supporting staff and involving families.

Chapters 4 through 6 highlight program areas that should be addressed by administrative review of policies, procedures, and planning. The ADA does not require anything that is harmful to children or overly burdensome for programs. Rather than asking if the law requires a specific accommodation, the authors hope that administrators of the programs will instead ask, "How can we find ways to include children with special needs so that everyone benefits?" We urge administrators to seek outside support and to be open to new ideas. Chapters 7 through 12 describe specific program changes and issues of concern for administrators. The appendixes at the end of the book explain terminology, provide resources, list pertinent case law, and provide forms pertaining to accessibility.

Summary

Making changes is challenging, but even simple changes can mean the difference between a successful experience and frustrated staff, children, and families. So we advise you to "just do it"—change the diaper, rearrange the room, modify the curriculum, reach out to families, and embrace complexity. Inclusion is not easy, but we believe the benefits are well worth the effort. We hope this book will help program administrators build strong partnerships with staff and families so that together they can create quality early learning environments for all children.

References

Americans with Disabilities Act of 1990, PL 101-336, 42 U.S.C. §§ 12101 *et seq.*
Annie E. Casey Foundation. (1998). *Kids count data book.* Baltimore: Author.
Bureau of Labor Statistics. (2006). *Employment characteristics of families.* Retrieved July 21, 2007, from http://www.bls.gov/new.release/famee.toc.htm
Child Care Plus. (2007). *Quality program = inclusive program.* Missoula: The University of Montana Rural Institute.
Children's Defense Fund. (1998). *Child care basics.* Retrieved July 5, 2002, from http://www.childrensdefensefund.org/cc_facts.htm
Mulligan, G.M., Brimhall, D., & West, J. (2005). *Child care and early education arrangement of infants, toddlers, and preschoolers: 2001* (NCES 2006-039). Washington, DC: U.S. Department of Education, National Center for Education Statistics, U.S. Government Printing Office.

National Child Care Resource and Referral Agencies (NACCRRA). (2006). *Child care in America.* Retrieved January 11, 2007, from http://www.naccrra.org/policy/docs

Pre[K]now. (2007). *Providing high-quality pre-k is a commitment to our children's future.* Retrieved August 11, 2008, from http://www.preknow.org

Shonkoff, J.P., & Phillips, D.A. (Eds.). (2000). *From neurons to neighborhoods.* Washington, DC: National Academies Press.

Urban Institute. (2004). *Nearly 3 out of 4 children of employed mothers are regularly in child care.* Washington, DC: Author.

U.S. Department of Education, Office of Special Education Programs. (2005). *History of the Individuals with Disabilities Education Act of 1990 (IDEA).* Washington, DC: Author.

I

Disability Laws and
Early Care and Education

1

Americans with Disabilities Act

> **Key Concepts:** auxiliary aids or services; direct
> threat; disability; discrimination; eligibility criteria;
> individuals with disabilities; integrated setting; major
> life activity; public entities; qualified individuals with
> disabilities; readily achievable; religious entity; undue
> burden; undue hardship

In 1990, Congress documented the need to protect the rights of people
with disabilities with the Americans with Disabilities Act (ADA) of 1990
(PL 101-336). They found that some 43 million Americans had physical
or mental disabilities and that this number is increasing as the population as a whole grows older.

(1) Historically, society had segregated and isolated those individuals
with disabilities and, despite some improvements, such forms of discrimination against individuals with disabilities continue to be a serious and pervasive social problem;

(2) Discrimination against individuals with disabilities persists in such
critical areas as employment, housing, public accommodations, education, transportation, communication, recreation, institutionaliza-
tion, health services, voting, and access to public services. (42 U.S.C.
§ 12101 [a])

Congress also noted that prior legislation to prevent **discrimination**
against **individuals with disabilities** did not sufficiently address and
remedy that discrimination. Section 504 of the Rehabilitation Act of 1973
(PL 93-112) had applied only to federally funded programs, so Congress

enacted the ADA to broaden the protections against discrimination in both the public and private sectors.

Through its five titles, the ADA prevents discrimination and guarantees equal opportunity to **qualified individuals with disabilities.**

Title I—*Employment:* To obtain employment based on abilities

Title II—*Public Services:* To receive services provided by state or local governments

Title III—*Public Accommodations:* To have access to public accommodations (e.g., facilities providing lodging, food, retail goods, medical, educational, and recreational services) and to obtain private and public transportation

Title IV—*Telecommunications:* To have the opportunity to use telecommunications

Title V—*Miscellaneous Provisions* (42 U.S.C. § 12101 *et seq.*)

Of these five titles, Titles II and Title III have the greatest impact on early childhood and are the focus of this book. Interestingly, the regulations for Title III were developed before those of Title II and were applied to Title II. This book adheres to the same order, with the discussion of Title III preceding the discussion of Title II.

The information presented here is not a substitute for legal advice. Early childhood program administrators may need specific legal information about how the ADA applies to their programs and should seek the assistance of attorneys who are familiar with ADA requirements.

Title III Public Accommodations

Title III of the ADA applies to private early childhood programs and the children and families they serve. Early childhood facilities are specifically included in the definition of public accommodations under Title III of the ADA:

> A facility, operated by a private entity, whose operations affect commerce and fall within at least one of the following categories
>
> J)   A nursery, elementary, secondary, undergraduate, or postgraduate private school, or other place of education;
>
> K)   A day care center, senior citizen center, or other social service center establishment. (42 U.S.C. § 12181 [7])

Hotels, restaurants, stores, museums, parks, and movie theaters are also examples of public accommodations.

This title contains a broad exemption for religious institutions and entities. Nursery schools and early childhood centers operated by churches are not subject to the requirements of the law (42 U.S.C. § 12187). For the religious exemption to apply, a **religious entity** must provide financial and/or administrative support to the early childhood program. But, if a church rents space to an independent child care center, then the law covers that center. If a church donates space to an early childhood center, however, then that center may be exempt from the law. Even though schools and centers run by religious institutions may be exempt from Title III of the ADA, other federal and state nondiscrimination laws may apply. For example, religious entities must still comply with Title I as it applies to their employees. Programs should check with their licensing agencies and state attorney general's offices to find out what other requirements apply to them.

Title II Public Services

Title III applies to public accommodations that are private entities whose goods and services are available to the public. Title II of the ADA invokes the same prohibitions against discrimination by **public entities,** which are "(A) any State or local government; (B) any department, agency, special purpose district, or other instrumentality of a State or States or local government" (42 U.S.C. § 12131 [1]). Title II covers all activities of state and local governments, including those that do not receive federal financial assistance. These public programs must be accessible and must communicate effectively with people with disabilities.

Some early childhood facilities are covered by both Title II for public programs and Title III for private programs, and the applicable title is not always easy to determine. The technical assistance manual for Title II lists several factors used to determine whether an entity is public or private:

1. Whether an entity operates with public funds

2. Whether employees are considered government employees

3. Whether the entity is governed by an independent board selected by members or a private organization or a board elected by the voters or appointed by elected officials (Civil Rights Division, 1993a)

If an entity is covered by both Titles II and III, then it must adhere to the highest standard.

Definition of Disability

The ADA defines **disability** in the following way:

> With respect to an individual, A) a physical or mental impairment that substantially limits one or more major life activities of such an individual; B) a record of such an impairment; or C) being regarded as having an impairment. (42 U.S.C. § 12102 [2])

Major life activities include caring for oneself, performing manual tasks, walking, seeing, hearing, speaking, breathing, learning, or working. These are the same definitions as those in Section 504 of the Rehabilitation Act of 1973.

In addition to people with disabilities, the ADA protects those who have a history of having an impairment. A child born with a heart defect that has been repaired is protected even though the child was incapacitated in the past. A third group protected by the law consists of people who are regarded as having an impairment even though they are not limited in any **major life activity.** For example, a child who was severely burned is not substantially limited in a major life activity, but her scars may cause people treat her as though she has a disability. The ADA protects her from discrimination. Finally, the ADA protects people who are associated with someone with a disability. For example, a child cannot be denied admission to an early childhood program because a parent or sibling has a disability. Some of the health conditions specifically protected under this broad definition of disability include cancer, human immunodeficiency virus (HIV), hepatitis B, and noncontagious tuberculosis.

Policy Prohibiting Discrimination

In general, public accommodations may not discriminate against people with disabilities. This means that children with disabilities must be given an opportunity to participate in public and private early childhood programs.

For private programs, the law states,

> No individual shall be discriminated against on the basis of disability in the full and equal enjoyment of the goods, services, facilities, privileges, advantages, or accommodations of any place of public accommodation by any person who owns, leases (or leases to), or operates a place of public accommodation. (42 U.S.C. § 12182 [a])

For public programs the law has similar requirements:

> No qualified individual with a disability shall, by reason of such disability, be excluded from participation in or be denied the benefits of the services,

programs, or activities of a public entity, or be subjected to discrimination by any such entity. (42 U.S.C. § 12132)

Participation of Individuals Who Do Not Have Disabilities

Early childhood programs must make provisions to ensure that children with disabilities can participate as much as possible in all program activities with their peers. Offering a separate program is usually not allowed because it could be viewed as an unequal service. The ADA prohibits the provision of unequal services, except when necessary to provide a service that is as effective for the individual with disabilities as that provided to others. This means that early childhood programs cannot deny services to a child with a disability even if a separate program is available specifically for children with disabilities. The law is clear on this point:

> Notwithstanding the existence of separate or different programs or activities provided in accordance with this subpart, a public accommodation shall not deny an individual with a disability an opportunity to participate in such programs or activities that are not separate or different. (42 U.S.C. § 12182 [2][1][C])

The issue in question is whether a separate program is necessary or appropriate for the individual. These provisions demonstrate that the ADA strongly encourages inclusive settings and discourages separate early childhood programs for children with disabilities.

Enforcement

There are two avenues for enforcement under Title II and Title III of the ADA. If a person feels that he or she has been discriminated against, then a civil action for injunctive relief may be filed. Parents may file suits on behalf of their children who are minors. In cases that rise to the level of general public importance, the U.S. Department of Justice may intervene in the civil action. In some situations, the court may also appoint an attorney for the plaintiff.

The U.S. Department of Justice will investigate allegations of Title II and Title III violations. An individual class of people who believe discrimination has occurred may request an investigation. If the U.S. Department of Justice has reason to believe that there may have been a violation of Title III, then it may initiate a compliance review.

If discrimination is found, then the person may be granted a permanent or temporary injunction or a restraining order. In effect, an early childhood program can be ordered by the court to make alterations related to accessibility, provide an **auxiliary aid or service,** or modify a policy. Furthermore, when a complaint is filed, the court takes into consideration any good faith efforts to comply with the law. This means that an honest effort to accommodate children will count in favor of any early childhood program that finds itself in court. The law does not include any compensatory or punitive monetary damages.

In cases in which a pattern of discrimination is verified or when the discrimination raises an issue of general public importance, the U.S. Department of Justice may bring a civil action. In this situation, monetary penalties also may apply. For a first violation, the court may assess a civil penalty not to exceed $50,000. Title III does not allow punitive damages.

Individuals may bring suit in a federal district court. The ADA is enforced by four agencies—the Equal Employment Opportunity Commission, U.S. Department of Justice, U.S. Department of Transportation, and the Federal Communications Commission—depending on the title to which the complaint applies. More detail about enforcement is provided in the third section of this chapter.

Specific Prohibitions

In addition to the general prohibitions of the law that address discrimination, four actions are specifically prohibited by the ADA. These actions are considered highly discriminatory, and if accommodations are not made, then violations may lead to litigation. These prohibitions are described and discussed in the following section. The four specific actions are[1]

(A) The imposition of eligibility criteria that screen out or tend to screen out an individual with a disability

(B) A failure to make reasonable modifications in policies, practices, or procedures when such modifications are necessary to afford such goods, services, facilities, privileges, advantages, or accommodations

(C) Failure to provide auxiliary aids and services

---

[1]The language of the law can be confusing. Statements are made about prohibiting an action rather than asserting what action is to be taken. To help clarify the application of the law, Chapter 2 will discuss litigation in early childhood programs prompted by the ADA and the outcomes. More importantly, the rest of the chapters will outline proactive steps to be taken to prepare early childhood programs to include young children with disabilities and comply with the law.

(D) Failure to remove architectural and communication barriers (42 U.S.C. § 12182 [2][A][a][i–iv])

Eligibility Criteria

Early childhood programs must have nondiscriminatory **eligibility criteria**. Specifically, the ADA prohibits the

> Imposition or application of eligibility criteria that screen out or tend to screen out an individual with a disability . . . from fully and equally enjoying any goods, services, facilities, advantages, and accommodations, unless such criteria can be shown to be necessary for the provision of the goods, services, facilities, privileges, advantages, or accommodations being offered. (42 U.S.C. § 12182 [b][2][A][I])

This means that admissions and enrollment criteria may not intentionally or unintentionally discriminate against children with disabilities. For example, if a program requires that children in the 3-year-old class be toilet trained, then this may unintentionally screen out children who cannot be toilet trained because of their disability. This eligibility criteria should be rewritten in nondiscriminatory language.

The one circumstance under which a program may have a restrictive policy is when a specific admission criterion is fundamental to the nature of the services being offered. Such criteria must be reviewed on a case-by-case basis. For example, a school for children who are gifted musically might require an audition to show that the applicant can sing in key and might reject any applicant who could not pass this test. If the school did not have this requirement, then it would substantially change the type of program it offered. Therefore, this restrictive admissions requirement probably would be allowed under the ADA. Such exemptions are rare, however, and usually do not apply to programs for young children. Many centers expect that all children in the 2-year-old group will be walking. Because walking is not fundamental to the nature of the services being offered, as a requirement for admission, this policy could discriminate against children with physical disabilities.

Reasonable Modifications in Policies, Practices, and Procedures

Early childhood programs are required to make "reasonable modifications in policies, practices, or procedures when such modifications are necessary to afford such goods, services, facilities, privileges, advantages, or accommodations to individuals with disabilities" (42 U.S.C. § 12182 [b][2][A][ii]).

These modifications must be **readily achievable,** that is, able to be made without **undue hardship** and expense. Early childhood programs must assess each potential change or modification and decide on a case-by-case basis which changes can be made. Factors to be considered include the needs of the child, the disability, the early childhood environment, and the resources of the program. Early childhood programs are not required to make modifications if they can demonstrate that "[modifications] would fundamentally alter the nature of such goods, services, facilities, privileges, or accommodations" (42 U.S.C. § 12182 [b][2][A][ii]).

This requirement of the ADA is closely tied to the purpose of the program and enrollment criteria of the program that are applied to all applicants. For example, a center-based early childhood program advertises its program as group care. To provide services to a child who required full-time, individual care would "fundamentally alter" the nature of their services.

Auxiliary Aids and Services

In addition to having nondiscriminatory eligibility criteria and making reasonable modifications to accommodate children with disabilities, early childhood programs must provide auxiliary aids and services and ensure effective communication for children with disabilities. Auxiliary aids and services assist people who have speech, learning, hearing, or visual impairments to communicate effectively. They can include sign language interpreters, written materials, assistive listening devices, notetakers, readers, taped texts, and braille or large-print materials. Provision of auxiliary aids and services is in keeping with the use of alternative methods for accessibility. As with reasonable modifications, early childhood programs must provide auxiliary aids and services unless doing so would fundamentally alter the nature of their program or would be an **undue burden.** Programs are not required to do things that involve significant difficulty or expense. Providing a sophisticated electronic communication device would prove an undue burden for most early childhood programs because of the expense.

Removal of Architectural and Communication Barriers for Accessibility

Under Title III, all early childhood programs are expected to make "readily achievable changes to physically accommodate those with disabilities by making existing facilities accessible and useable. When barrier removal is not readily achievable, the entity must still make its goods,

Final Brief Topic and Essential Question

Name: _Jessa Gagarin_

Topic: _Discrimination Against People who with Disabilities in School_

Essential Question: _What types of adjustments are required for students with disabilities in k-12 schools?_

Topic and Essential Question Approval: _[signature]_ Date: _11/05/15._

and services . . . available through alternative methods" (42 U.S.C. § 12182 [b][2][A] [iv–v]). Each program must look at its own resources and the changes required. Decisions are made on a case-by-case basis. Accommodations that are readily achievable for a large corporate early childhood program might be unrealistic for a small neighborhood program.

Factors[2] that the law considers when deciding if removal of a physical barrier is readily achievable include

A) The nature and cost of the action
B) The overall financial resources of the site or sites involved
C) Legitimate safety requirements necessary for safe operation
D) If applicable, the overall financial resources of any parent corporation or entity (42 U.S.C. § 12181 [9][A])

A major difference between Title II and Title III is the requirement for program accessibility. The regulation from Title II regarding accessibility states, "a public entity shall operate each service, program, or activity so that the service, program, or activity, when viewed in its entirety, is readily accessible to and usable by individuals with disabilities" (28 C.F.R. § 35.150). This means that a public entity is required to make its programs accessible, but it is not required to make each of its existing facilities accessible. This program accessibility requirement is required in all cases, except when it would result in a fundamental alteration of the nature of the program or would be an *undue financial and administrative burden*. This requirement differs from Title III, which requires private entities to make each facility accessible.

Congress intended the undue burden standard in Title II to be significantly higher than the readily achievable standard in Title III (Civil Rights Division, 1993b). Title II does not require removal of barriers in some cases. The program access requirement of Title II should enable individuals with disabilities to participate in and benefit from the services, programs, or activities of public entities in all but the most unusual cases. Public entities may use either Uniform Federal Accessibility Standards (UFAS), the regulations developed for Section 504 of the Rehabilitation Act of 1973, or the Americans with Disabilities Act Accessibility Guidelines (ADAAG) when making renovations to existing facilities or when constructing new facilities.

---

[2]It should be noted that the undue burden standard that applies to the provision of auxiliary aids and services requires a greater level of effort than does the readily achievable standard for removing physical barriers in existing facilities. Even though the standards are different, the factors to be considered in determining what qualifies as an undue burden are identical to those listed previously for determining what is readily achievable (Civil Rights Division, 1993b).

The federal government is beginning to address the access needs of children more directly. New accessibility guidelines for children's play areas appeared in the *Federal Register* and were effective November 17, 2000 (ADAAG for Buildings, Facilities, and Play Areas, 2000). Although these guidelines are available for any new construction or renovation, they are not enforceable until adopted by the U.S. Department of Justice.

The four prohibitions of the ADA ensure equal access to early childhood programs for children with disabilities. Title II and Title III, however, do allow exclusion of children with disabilities in two situations: 1) **direct threat** and 2) fundamental alteration of the nature of the program. With these criteria in mind, an early childhood program must assess its ability to meet the particular needs of any child at the time the child applies to the program.

The term *direct threat* means a significant risk to the health or safety of others that cannot be eliminated by a modification of policies, practices, or procedures or by the provision of auxiliary aids or services (42 U.S.C. § 12182 [3]). An early childhood program is not required to allow an individual to participate in the program who poses a direct threat. The exclusion for direct threat to the health and safety of others, however, cannot be invoked based on beliefs about what children with disabilities can and cannot do, how much assistance they may need, or assertions of others. To invoke the direct threat exclusion after a child has been admitted, the early childhood program must document the issue of concern, the measures it has taken to provide a program for the child with modifications and auxiliary aids and services, and the continued presence of danger.

An early childhood program may also exclude a child with a disability if the admission of that child would require a *fundamental alteration of the nature of the program* (42 U.S.C. § 12182 [b][2][A][ii]). An example of fundamental alteration of programming was shown in *Roberts v. KinderCare Learning Centers, Inc* (1995, 1996). In order to attend an early childhood program, Roberts, the plaintiff, needed one-to-one supervision. The lawyer for the defendant argued that early childhood programs provide group care, not individual care. The court ruled in favor of KinderCare.

Summary

The ADA is the most comprehensive legislation to eliminate discrimination against individuals with disabilities. It retains the definition of disability from Section 504 of the Rehabilitation Act of 1973 and the support for integrated settings. Titles II and III of the ADA extend Section 504's previous prohibitions of discrimination in federally funded programs to state and local governments and the private sector. These two titles also outline four specific prohibitions against discrimination. Pursuant to these two titles of the ADA, public and private programs must have 1) nondiscriminatory eligibility criteria, 2) reasonable modifications in policies, practices, and procedures for individuals with disabilities, 3) auxiliary aids and services available, and 4) architectural and communication barriers removed.

2

Enforcement
of the Americans
with Disabilities Act in
Early Childhood Programs

> **Key Concepts:** nondiscrimination policy; physical
> accessibility; public accommodation; reasonable
> modifications

This chapter summarizes the litigation in early childhood programs related to Title III of the ADA.

Actions by the U.S. Department of Justice

The U.S. Department of Justice views child care as an important **public accommodation** for implementation of the ADA. The U.S. Department of Justice publishes a resource fact sheet and a set of questions and answers for child care providers containing general information about the ADA: who it covers; what personal services it covers; what issues for specific disabilities, such as HIV and allergies, it covers; and how to make a child care center accessible. In the 10th anniversary report, *Enforcing the ADA: Looking Back on a Decade of Progress* (2000), and *Access for All: Five Years of Progress* (2006), the U.S. Department of Justice devoted sections to its cases involving early childhood programs that have been filed, settled, and adjudicated. In several cases, the U.S. Department of Justice filed *amici curiae*[1] briefs supporting plaintiffs.

Most of the cases address **reasonable modifications** and eligibility criteria in policies that need to be made so children with disabilities can attend early childhood programs.

The U.S. Department of Justice also provides technical assistance on the implementation of the law. When individuals make inquiries, the U.S. Department of Justice responds with core letters or letters of technical assistance, which provide guidance but do not set legal precedent. The Freedom of Information Act (FOIA) of 1966 (PL 85-619) makes these letters a matter of public record, and they are available to the public by request or on the ADA web site (see http://www.ada.gov). To date, the U.S. Department of Justice has written several letters addressing issues in early childhood programs. Specific inquiries related to early childhood programs include 1) the admission of children who are HIV positive and denial of insurance coverage, 2) whether a religious exemption pertains if no lease exists for an early childhood center housed in a religious facility, 3) the ADA obligations of an early childhood center if space is leased rather than owned, 4) whether a toilet-training requirement is disallowed, and 5) charging extra fees for children with disabilities who require additional time and care.

When an individual believes that his or her rights have been violated under Titles II or III of the ADA, he or she can file an administrative complaint with the U.S. Department of Justice. Parents or primary caregivers would file on behalf of a child. The U.S. Department of Justice determines if an investigation is warranted. If the complaint is investigated, then the agency can issue a Letter of Findings and attempt to reach a resolution of differences. Determinations and resolutions do not set legal precedent but provide guidance on the issue. When an individual files an ADA claim, a court may require that a plaintiff exhaust administrative remedies before hearing the case.

Summary of Case Law[2]

At the same time an administrative complaint is made to the U.S. Department of Justice, a suit can be filed in court. A case is filed first in the Federal District Court[3] in the judicial district in which the case arises. Any

---

[1]An *amicus curiae* brief (plural: *amici curiae*) is written in support of a plaintiff or defendant by a group or institution with no standing in the case, but with a vested interest in the outcome.

[2]Case law is a form of law. Congress creates statutory law. The administrative agency designated by Congress creates regulatory law. The written opinion of judges that set legal precedent is case law.

[3]A district is a relatively small geographic area of a circuit. There are 13 circuits in the United States.

decision rendered in that court is binding only in that district. If the plaintiff is not satisfied with the court decision, then he or she has the right to appeal the decision. The Appellate, or Circuit, Court hears appeals. Any decision rendered in the Appellate Court is binding only in that circuit. The final court of appeal is the U.S. Supreme Court, and its decision is binding anywhere in the United States.

A summary of cases filed in the courts gives an indication of the prohibitions of the ADA that have prompted disputes with child care programs and, perhaps, have been problematic for the implementation of the law. Several cases have been brought at the District Court level. In all but one case, either confidential or public settlements have been reached prior to trial. Only *Roberts v. KinderCare Learning Centers, Inc.* (1995, 1996) ended with an Appellate Court decision. Cases related to Titles II and III have been heard by the Supreme Court, but cases involving early childhood programs have not gone to that court.

The following summary of cases is organized by the components of the law that have precipitated the most litigation.

Reasonable Modifications

The specific requirement for reasonable modifications in policies, practices, and procedures has resulted in many cases on behalf of children who require procedures related to health conditions, such as a fingerprick test for diabetes, the administration of medication for allergies, or the use of an EpiPen for life-threatening allergies (*Alvarez v. Fountainhead*, 1999; *Breen v. State of Connecticut, Department of Public Health and Addiction Services*, 1994; *Stuthard v. KinderCare Learning Centers, Inc.*, 1996). Defendants have settled these cases, and there were no resulting legal precedents. Centers modified policies to accommodate the child with disabilities pursuant to the settlement agreements. KinderCare Learning Centers, a nationwide child care chain, has implemented comprehensive policies and procedures controlling the administration of the glucose finger-prick test and the EpiPen. *E.M. v. Town Sports International, Inc., and TSI Wellesley, Inc.* (2006), prompted modifications in policy to monitor blood glucose testing and administration of insulin. Such procedures have been problematic in some states, such as Connecticut and California, due to state regulations that prohibit early childhood staff from administering health-related procedures.

Program modifications about the kind of care a child requires and subsequent accommodations have prompted additional cases (*Ireland v. Kansas District of the Wesleyan Church*, 1994; *Orr v. KinderCare Learning Centers, Inc.*, 1995; *Roberts v. KinderCare Learning Centers, Inc.*, 1996). Families of children with disabilities asked the federal courts to determine whether early childhood programs made reasonable modifications for the children with disabilities attending their centers. In three cases, the centers prohibited children who were not ambulatory or toilet trained from moving into the next appropriate group for care. In one case, a state safety requirement stated that all children in the toddler groups must be ambulatory. The majority of the cases have been settled, and these settlements require that programs make the requested accommodations. Although there are no binding decisions, the trend seems to be in favor of centers making the changes needed to accommodate the children who are considered qualified individuals with disabilities under the law.

One case did not end in settlement, but it ended in a court decision that denied one-to-one assistance for a child with extensive needs. The District Court ruled that a modification for one-to-one care would fundamentally alter the nature of the provision of group care. This decision in favor of the child care program was upheld by the Circuit Court of Appeals (*Roberts v. KinderCare Learning Centers, Inc.*, 1996). By contrast, a case brought in the Ninth Circuit Court reached a different result (*Orr v. KinderCare Learning Centers, Inc.*, 1995). In this case, the child's parents provided a one-to-one assistant, but the center still wished to exclude the child. Under the settlement agreement, the child was permitted to attend the child care program with his aide. The differing decisions underscore the unique factors in the provision of accommodations, such as the needs of the child, the type and extent of the disability, the environment, and the disposition of that District Court. The courts consider the circumstances of each case on an individual basis.

Other factors affect whether suits are brought and what programmatic changes are required by defendants. When complaints by multiple plaintiffs are made, the reason to investigate a possible *pattern* of discrimination is greater than for a single incident. The nature and costs of the modifications in relation to the resources of the public accommodation is another factor in determining the extent of the modifications required. The ADA permits courts to demand more modifications from programs with a larger financial base than from small programs with fewer resources. Modifications are not required that would fundamentally alter the nature of the program. Accessibility barriers must be removed if they are readily achievable and do not pose an undue burden. For example, an early childhood program that is part of a large parent corporation may well have resources that are greater than a small, independent center.

Several complaints and suits were brought against a nationwide chain, KinderCare Learning Centers (e.g., *Orr v. KinderCare Learning Centers, Inc.*, 1995; *Roberts v. KinderCare Learning Centers, Inc.*, 1995, 1996). Both an implied pattern of discrimination and greater resources may have been reasons that the U.S. Department of Justice got involved and for the requirements of the settlement. The settlements required KinderCare to write and implement extensive new policies and procedures. KinderCare now employs a disabilities coordinator who is involved in all decision making regarding children with disabilities.

Eligibility Criteria

Imposing eligibility criteria that screen out children with disabilities has been the second most contested area of concern under the ADA. Admission of children with HIV was the cause of two cases: *Morrell v. Mexican American Opportunity Foundation* (Child Care Law Center, 1997), and *U.S. v. Kiddie Ranch, Happy Time, and ABC Playhouse* (1997). In the case of *U.S. v. Joetta Roberts*, the Morrell case, the center refused to admit a child whose mother had died of AIDS unless he was tested for HIV. The ADA is very clear that children cannot be refused care based on their HIV status or the HIV status of someone closely associated with them (Gil de Lamadrid, 1996). In the case of *U.S. v. Joetta Roberts*, a child was refused admission because his mother was being treated for hepatitis C status (*Enforcing the ADA, Part 2*, n.d.). The suit was settled, the center was required to adopt a **nondiscrimination policy,** and staff were required to attend training on the obligations for child care providers under the ADA. In the suits against Kiddie Ranch, Happy Time, and ABC Playhouse, the centers refused admission to a child who was HIV positive and argued that the child was not disabled. The District Court judge ruled that this case should be brought to trial, and the U.S. Department of Justice represented the child. The child care centers have now agreed that a child who is HIV positive is disabled under the ADA. The child care programs settled the case and agreed to sponsor an informational meeting for interested child care providers, parents, and staff to discuss the ADA and HIV.

The admission requirement to be toilet trained is another contested eligibility criterion in programs. Suits brought against Head Start programs have been settled. Helen Taylor, the Associate Director of Head Start issued a memorandum stating that programs "should not deny enrollment to a child on the basis of toileting skills, regardless of whether or not that child has a disability" (H. Taylor, personal communication, 1995). A 4-year-old child with Down syndrome was denied admission because the center had a policy requiring that a child be toilet trained by age 3 in the case of *U.S. v. Peggy's Child Care* (*Enforcing the ADA, Part 2*, n.d.). The center was required to modify its policy to exempt children with disabilities from the toilet-training criteria and require staff training about the ADA (*Enforcing the ADA, Part 2*, n.d.).

Physical Accessibility

Lack of **physical accessibility** has been cited as a barrier to including children with disabilities in child care programs (Child Care Bureau, 1995; Richey, Richey, & Webb, 1996; Wolery et al., 1993a; Wolery et al., 1993b). Increased physical access to child care programs can be achieved by removing barriers and making physical changes, such as alterations to buildings, playgrounds, and classroom environments. Portions of existing facilities under renovation and any new construction must be made fully accessible. New construction and alterations to existing facilities must adhere to the ADAAG.[4]

Auxiliary Aids and Services

Only one case has involved the provision of auxiliary aids and services. Extended Love Child Development, a center in Wisconsin, agreed to provide qualified sign language interpreters or auxiliary aids and services to deaf and hard-of-hearing children (and parents, if they are also deaf and hard of hearing) in communication-intensive activities. The center also agreed to provide staff training on communicating with individuals with hearing disabilities (U.S. Department of Justice, 2003).

As demonstrated in this case, the courts invoked four specific prohibitions of the law:

1. The prohibition against failure to make reasonable modifications in policies, practices, and procedures to accommodate children with disabilities

2. The prohibition against eligibility criteria that tend to screen out children with disabilities

3. The prohibition against the failure to remove accessibility barriers

4. The prohibition against the failure to provide auxiliary aids and services

The majority of cases have been settled in favor of the family making the complaint and have confirmed the need for appropriate accommodations, nondiscriminatory eligibility criteria, physical accessibility, and auxiliary aids and services in child care programs. For a summary of complaints and specific cases, see Appendix C at the end of the book.

---

[4]The regulations of the ADA detail a wide range of administrative and procedural requirements, including compliance with design and construction standards developed by the Architectural and Transportation Barriers Compliance Board (Access Board).

3

Other Disability Laws that Affect the Presence of Children in Early Childhood Programs

> **Key Concepts:** accommodation; barrier free; due process procedure; eligibility; individualized education program (IEP); individualized family service plan (IFSP); least restrictive environment (LRE); natural environment; related service; special education

Until the 1970s, children with disabilities often were denied access to public education. The civil rights movement, advocacy for people with disabilities, and the efforts of parents of children with disabilities contributed to the passage of two laws that ensured the rights of children with disabilities, mandated **accommodations,** and provided **special education** services.

Section 504 of the Rehabilitation Act of 1973 provides access to educational programs receiving federal funds and is the source of much of the language of the ADA. The Education for All Handicapped Children Act of 1975 (PL 94-142) and the Individuals with Disabilities Education Act (IDEA) of 1990 (PL 101-476) and its subsequent amendments (1991 [PL 102-119], 1997 [PL 105-17], and 2004 [108-446]) mandate education for children with disabilities in public schools.

Rehabilitation Act of 1973

When Section 504 of the Rehabilitation Act of 1973 was passed, it was landmark legislation that prohibited discrimination against individuals with disabilities by recipients of federal financial assistance, including early care and education programs. "Section 504 transformed federal disability policy by conceptualizing access for people with disabilities as a civil right rather than a welfare benefit" (National Council on Disability, 1997, p. 20). Much of the language and intent of this law has been carried into the ADA.

Although the law was passed in 1973, the regulations for the implementation of Section 504 were strongly debated and were not completed until 1977. The regulations defined disability, delineated prohibited discriminatory action, established construction standards, and instituted educational policies. These regulations provided the foundation for many concepts found in the ADA.

Definition of Disability

The Rehabilitation Act of 1973 defines a person with a disability as any person who

(i)   Has a physical or mental impairment which substantially limits one or more of such person's major life activities

(ii)   Has a record of such an impairment

(iii)   Is regarded as having such an impairment (29 U.S.C. § 706 [8][B])

Major life activities include caring for oneself, performing manual tasks, seeing, hearing, speaking, breathing, learning, and walking (34 C.F.R. § 104). Section 504 applies to people with disabilities of all ages, including children. The definition and explanation remain the same in the ADA.

Policy Prohibiting Discrimination

At the time, the Rehabilitation Act of 1973 represented a tremendous breakthrough in the civil rights of people with disabilities because it specifically prohibits discrimination. The law states the following:

> No otherwise qualified individual with a disability shall, solely by reason of her or his disability, be excluded from the participation in, be denied the benefits of, or otherwise be subjected to discrimination under any program or activity receiving Federal financial assistance. (29 U.S.C. § 794)

In addition, the regulations for Section 504 include specific language about early childhood programs:

> A recipient that operates a preschool education or day care program or activity or an adult education program or activity may not, on the basis of handicap, exclude qualified handicapped persons from the program or activity and shall take into account the needs of such persons in determining the aid, benefits, or services to be provided under the program or activity. (45 C.F.R. § 84.38)

In programs and activities that receive federal assistance, Section 504 requires equal and accessible transportation, architecture, educational programs, and nonacademic services for children and adults with disabilities.

Participation of Individuals Who Do Not Have Disabilities

The regulations of Section 504 of the Rehabilitation Act of 1973 encourage individuals with and without disabilities to participate in the same academic and nonacademic educational settings.

1. *Academic setting.* A recipient to which this subpart applies shall educate, or shall provide for the education of each qualified handicapped person in its jurisdiction with persons who are not handicapped to the maximum extent appropriate to the need of the handicapped person. A recipient shall place a handicapped person in the regular educational environment operated by the recipient unless it is demonstrated by the recipient that the education of the person in the regular environment with the use of supplementary aids and services cannot be achieved satisfactorily.

2. *Nonacademic settings.* In placing or arranging for the provision of nonacademic and extracurricular services and activities, including meals, recess periods, and the service and activities set for the 84.37(a)(2), a recipient shall ensure that handicapped persons participate with non-handicapped persons in such activities and services to the maximum extent appropriate to the needs of the handicapped person in question. (45 C.F.R. § 84.34)

Any early childhood programs receiving federal assistance, such as those on military bases and those administered by the General Services Administration (GSA) programs in federal buildings, may not discriminate against children, families, or employees with disabilities. As illustrated in the previous regulations, Section 504 encourages integrated programs in which individuals with and without disabilities receive services and participate in the same program (45 C.F.R. § 84.34). Programs must provide supplemental aids and services to help achieve this participation. All of the physical facilities (e.g., entrances, corridors, classrooms, play spaces, bathrooms) must be accessible and **barrier free.** Any transportation provided, such as buses or vans, must also be accessible for all users.

When it is necessary to provide separate services, the quality of those services cannot be substantially different. Both programs must provide services of equal quality. Different treatment is justified only if it is necessary to provide services to people with disabilities that are as effective as those provided to others. Individuals with disabilities are encouraged to participate as much as possible in programs with their peers without disabilities. In cases in which there are separate programs, a person with a disability cannot be forced to participate in one program or the other but has the right to participate in either program. This law encourages individuals with and without disabilities to participate together.

Enforcement

Section 504 of the Rehabilitation Act of 1973 outlines due process rights for individuals with disabilities. Any programs that have discriminatory practices may face litigation and loss of federal funds, even if the funding is through indirect support. For example, if an early childhood program participates in a federal food program, participation in the food program would be in jeopardy if the program discriminates against children or employees with disabilities.

Because Section 504 was a precursor to, and the basis for, the ADA, early childhood facilities that comply with Section 504 already have many of the components in place to meet the requirements of the ADA. Section 504 defines a person with a disability, prohibits discrimination against people with disabilities, encourages programs to serve individuals with and without disabilities in academic and nonacademic settings, and establishes **due process procedures** for enforcement.

Education for All Handicapped Children Act of 1975

Until 1975, children with disabilities had no legal right to a public education. In 1975, the Education for All Handicapped Children Act of 1975 was passed and required public schools to offer all eligible children with disabilities a free appropriate public education (FAPE; 20 U.S.C. § 1400 [c]) and provided federal assistance for that purpose. Initially, Section

Table 3.1. Major amendments to the Individuals with Disabilities Education Act (IDEA) and related legislation since 1986

Date	Number	Changes
1986	PL 99-457	The Education of the Handicapped Act Amendments of 1986 lowered the age of eligibility for special education and related services for children with disabilities from age 5 to age 3.
		The amendments also established a discretionary program (Part H) for infants and toddlers with disabilities, birth through 2 years, and their families.
1990	PL 101-476	The Individuals with Disabilities Education Act (IDEA) of 1990 amended the Education of the Handicapped Act Amendments of 1986.
1997	PL 105-17	The IDEA 1997 amendments renamed Part H as Part C. Both the 1997 amendments and the subsequent 1999 regulations strengthened the provision of services to young children in *natural environments* (i.e., the location where a child might be if he or she did not have a disability). For example, a natural environment might be a child's home, an early childhood program, or a family child care home.
2004	PL 108-446	This is referred to as the Individuals with Disabilities Education Improvement Act (IDEA 2004).
		The regulations for Part B have been published. The notice for the proposed regulations (34 C.F.R. 303 *et seq.*) for Part C was published May 7, 2007.

619, Part B of the Education for All Handicapped Children Act of 1975 provided preschool grants for children ages 3–5. A series of amendments lowered the age of **eligibility** and established a program for infants and toddlers. IDEA 2004 now covers children from birth through 22 in all states. Table 3.1 shows major changes to IDEA throughout the years.

Each state is responsible for developing a plan to ensure it meets the requirements of the law. Each state must ensure that

- All children with disabilities, regardless of the severity of their disability, receive a FAPE at public expense.

- The education of children with disabilities is based on a complete and individual evaluation and assessment of specific, unique needs of each child.

- An **individualized education program (IEP)** or an **individualized family service plan (IFSP)** is drawn up for every child found eligible for special education or early intervention services, stating precisely what types of special education and **related services,** or the types of early intervention services, each child will receive.

- All children with disabilities are educated in the regular education environment to the maximum extent possible.

- Eligible children have the right to receive related services necessary to benefit from special education instruction.

- Parents have the right to participate in every decision related to the identification, evaluation, and placement of their children.

- There must be parental consent for any initial evaluation, assessment, or placement. Parents must be notified of any change in placement that may occur; must be included, along with teachers, in conferences and meetings held to draw up individualized programs; and must approve these plans before they go into effect.

- Parents have the right to challenge and appeal any decision related to identification, evaluation, and placement or any issue concerning the provision of FAPE to their child. These rights are spelled out clearly in due process procedures.

- Parents have the right to have information kept confidential. No one may see a child's records unless the parents give their written permission. The exception to this is school personnel with legitimate education interests (Osborne & DiMattia, 1994).

Definition of Disability

Under IDEA 2004, children ages 3–21 are eligible if they have disabilities that warrant special education and related services. The definition of disability under IDEA is quite different from the definition of disability in Section 504. Under IDEA, *disability* is defined specifically according to a diagnosis that adversely affects educational performance for a child. The descriptions by category are as follows.

1. *Autism* is a developmental disability that significantly affects verbal and nonverbal communication and social interaction. It is a neurological disorder. Autism's onset is often recognized between 18 months and 4 years of age. Other characteristics often associated with autism are engagement in repetitive activities and stereotyped movements, resistance to environmental change or change in daily routines, and unusual responses to sensory experiences.

2. *Deafness* is a hearing impairment that is so severe that a child is unable to hear and understand spoken words, with or without amplification.

3. *Deaf-blindness* means concomitant hearing and visual impairments, the combination of which causes such severe communication and other developmental and educational problems that they cannot be accommodated in special education programs solely for children with blindness.

4. *Hearing impairment* means that an individual has a hearing loss, whether permanent or fluctuating.

5. *Mental retardation* is significantly below average general intellectual functioning existing concurrently with deficits in adaptive behavior. Adaptive behavior refers to the ability to meet the demands of the environment through age-appropriate, independent skills in self-care, communication, and play.

6. *Multiple disabilities* means concomitant impairments, such as mental retardation–blindness, mental retardation–orthopedic impairment, and so forth, the combination of which causes such severe educational problems that they cannot be accommodated in a program solely for one of the impairments.

7. *Orthopedic impairment* is any condition that involves muscles, bones, or joints and is characterized by difficulty with movement. The term includes impairments caused by congenital anomaly (e.g., clubfoot, absence of a body limb), impairments caused by disease (e.g., poliomyelitis, bone tuberculosis), and impairments from other causes (e.g., cerebral palsy, amputations, fractures or burns that cause contractures.) It affects the ability to perform small or large muscle activities or to perform self-help skills in educational or noneducational settings.

8. *Other health impairment* is a condition that limits strength, vitality, or alertness due to a chronic or acute health problem. Examples are cancer, some neurological disorders, rheumatic fever, severe asthma, uncontrolled seizure disorders, heart conditions, lead poisoning, diabetes, AIDS, blood disorders (hemophilia, sickle cell anemia), cystic fibrosis, heart disease, and attention-deficit/hyperactivity disorder (ADHD).

9. *Severe emotional disturbance*[1] describes a child who has behavioral or emotional responses that are extremely different from other children with the same ethnic or cultural background. These extreme behaviors impair social relationships and self-care skills and are very disruptive in the classroom.

> (i) The term means a condition that includes one or more of the following characteristics over a long period of time and to a marked degree that adversely affects a child's educational performance.
>
> A) An inability to learn that cannot be explained by intellectual, sensory, or health factors

---

[1]It is unusual for young children to be given this diagnosis. Usually, extreme behaviors in young children are related to autism, mental retardation, acquired brain injury (ABI), or general developmental delay. Sometimes these behaviors result from early trauma, such as abuse or neglect.

> B) An inability to build or maintain satisfactory inter-personal relationships with peers and teachers
>
> C) Inappropriate types of behavior or feelings under normal circumstances
>
> D) A general pervasive mood of unhappiness or depression
>
> E) A tendency to develop physical symptoms or fears associated with personal or school problems
>
> (ii) The term includes schizophrenia. The term does not apply to children who are socially maladjusted, unless it is determined that they have a serious emotional disturbance.

10. *Specific learning disability*[2] is a disorder in one or more of the basic *psychological* processes involved in understanding or using spoken or written language. Children may have difficulty listening, thinking, speaking, writing, spelling, or doing mathematical calculations. The term includes such conditions as perceptual disabilities, brain injury, minimal brain dysfunction, dyslexia, and developmental aphasia. The term does not apply to children who have learning problems that are primarily the result of visual, hearing, or motor disabilities; mental retardation; emotional disturbance; or environmental, cultural, or economic disadvantage. Although this definition does not usually apply to preschool-age children, teachers may notice children who have trouble acquiring the *beginning* skills for reading, writing, spelling, or doing math.

11. *Speech or language impairments* are communication disorders, such as stuttering, impaired articulation, or voice impairment. This category also includes the inability to express oneself or an inability to understand what is being said.

12. *Traumatic brain injury* (TBI)[3] is an injury to the brain caused by an external physical force, resulting in total or partial functional disability or psychosocial impairment or both. The term applies to open or closed head injuries resulting in impairments in one or more areas, such as cognition; language; memory; attention; reasoning; abstract thinking; judgment; problem solving; sensory, perceptual, and motor abilities;

---

[2]This category is very broad and it may be difficult to distinguish a learning disability from other learning problems especially in a young child. Each school system develops its own criteria for determining if a child has a learning disability. Contact your local special education department in the public school for their definition.

[3]Although the preferred terminology for this disability has been changed to ABI, *traumatic brain injury (TBI)* is the term used in IDEA.

psychosocial behavior; physical functions; information processing; and speech. The term does not apply to brain injuries that are congenital or degenerative or induced by birth trauma.

13. *Visual impairment* is any loss of sight that, with or without correction, adversely affects a child's learning. *Blindness* refers to a condition with no vision or only light perception. *Low vision* refers to limited distance vision or the ability to see only items close to the eyes.

In addition to these categories, IDEA 2004 has revised the definition for young children with developmental delay. *Developmental delay* is now defined as children ages birth to 9 years who are experiencing delays, as defined by their state, and measured by appropriate diagnostic instruments and procedures in one or more of the following areas: physical development, cognitive development, communication development, social or emotional development, or adaptive development and who therefore need education and related services (34 C.F.R. 300.8).

The extent of the delays may range from mild to severe. The delays may include

1. Children with identifiable conditions that interfere with their learning and development
2. Children with developmental delays but no apparent biological condition
3. Children who are at risk because of a variety of environmental and/or biological factors

Policy Prohibiting Discrimination

No child who meets these categorical definitions and a state's eligibility criteria may be denied a FAPE in accordance with the requirements of IDEA 2004.

Least Restrictive Environment

One of the requirements of IDEA 2004, Part B, is that **special education** and related services for children ages 3 and older must be provided in the **least restrictive environment (LRE)**. LRE refers to the legal principle that children with disabilities are to be educated in an environment as close as possible to the general education environment (Osborne & Dimattia, 1994). IDEA 2004 ensures that

1. To the maximum extent appropriate, children with disabilities are educated with children who are not disabled.
2. Special classes, separate schooling, or other removal of children with disabilities from the regular educational environment occurs only

when the nature or severity of the disability is such that education in regular classes with the use of supplementary aids and services cannot be achieved satisfactorily. (34 C.F.R. § 300.550 [b])

This legal principle also appears in Section 504 regulations that discourage separate settings. IDEA allows children to be removed from general education only when absolutely necessary. School districts must have a continuum of alternative placements available to children who are eligible for special education.

Natural Environments

Children with disabilities who qualify under Part C, the early intervention program for infants and toddlers, receive services in their **natural environment** (i.e., the location where the child would be if he or she did not have a disability). Services can be provided in the home, in early childhood programs, or in recreation facilities.

Although public school systems provide special education services for preschool-age children with disabilities, many public school systems do not offer educational services for preschool-age children without disabilities. Therefore, educators and parents have begun to seek and use community early childhood programs, Head Start programs, and child care programs as less restrictive alternatives to segregated preschool programs that serve only children with disabilities. The growing emphasis on serving infants, toddlers, and preschoolers in natural and LREs (Hyson, 1998; Stainback & Stainback, 1996) means that early childhood program administrators need to be familiar with the rights of children with disabilities. Early childhood program administrators must learn about the special education process, service provision, and accommodations that are necessary to make their programs accessible.

Enforcement

Parents must be given information about their due process rights at each decision-making point in the process of eligibility for special education. These due process rights are the same as those in Section 504 of the Rehabilitation Act of 1973. The enforcing agencies are the state and local education agencies and the U.S. Department of Education.

Summary of Federal Legislation

Section 504 of the Rehabilitation Act of 1973, IDEA 2004, and the ADA all define an eligible person with a disability, prohibit discrimination against individuals with disabilities, ensure equal rights under the law, and de-

Table 3.2. Comparison of the laws

	Individuals with Disabilities Education Act	Rehabilitation Act of 1973 Section 504	Americans with Disabilities Act Titles II and III
Setting	Least restrictive environment	Supports integrated settings and use of segregated programs only as necessary	Supports integrated settings and use of segregated settings only if necessary
Definition of disability	Specific disabling conditions defined	General and comprehensive definition of disability and qualified individual with a disability	General and comprehensive definition of disability and qualified individual with a disability (same as Section 504)
Applies to	Public education	Federally funded programs and activities services	State and local government Public accommodations
Enforcement	Office of Special Education Programs, U.S. Department of Education	Disability Rights Section, Civil Rights Division, U.S. Department of Justice	U.S. Department of Justice

scribe appropriate programming for children and adults with disabilities. Each of the three laws applies to programs under different auspices. Section 504 applies to federally supported programs and activities. IDEA 2004 applies to public education programs. The ADA applies to programs and facilities of state and local governments and the private sector. Early childhood programs that receive federal funds serve as natural environments for children eligible under IDEA. These programs are under the auspices of state and local governments. These public accommodations in the private sector must adhere to the same prohibitions. These early childhood programs must make the required accommodations for children with disabilities and must ensure that children with disabilities can participate in all program activities with their peers to the maximum extent possible. Table 3.2 summarizes the three laws by setting, definition of disability, the applicable program, and enforcement agency.

II

Administrative Components

This section discusses modifications in policies and provides examples of reasonable modifications in programming, auxiliary aids and services, and physical accessibility. The information in this section is based on litigated issues, technical assistance documents from the U.S. Department of Justice, and research on high-quality early childhood environments.

4

Components of High-Quality,
Americans with Disabilities
Act–Compliant Programs

Key Concepts: chronological placement; dual placement; full participation; fundamental alteration; nondiscrimination statement

---

This chapter provides an administrator with the information to design and conduct a program review to ensure compliance with the law and its regulations. This self-review process is similar to other self-assessments, such as a review for licensing standards, the self-study for the National Association for the Education of Young Children (NAEYC) accreditation (2006), an examination of the physical and learning environment using the Early Childhood Environmental Rating Scale–Revised (ECERS-R; Harms, Clifford, & Cryer, 2005), the Infant/Toddler Environmental Rating Scale– Revised (ITERS-R; Harms, Clifford, & Cryer, 2003), or the Program Administration Scale (PAS; Talan & Bloom, 2004). The goal of conducting such a review is not only simply to comply with the law but also to ensure high quality of programming. To make sure that the program meets the needs of children with disabilities, the review should examine 1) the program policies, procedures, and written materials distributed to the public; 2) the learning environment (e.g., schedule, curriculum, classroom activities); and 3) the physical environment. The results of prior litigation highlight specific program areas and changes required by the courts. In addition to providing suggestions to avoid litigation, this chapter also provides suggestions for practices that support quality in early childhood environments.

Policies and Procedures

Programs need written policies and procedures to guide how they operate and how administrators make program decisions. Some programs have formal, written policies and procedures and a shorter, edited version in the form of a parent handbook. Some programs use only a parent handbook. Most programs also have an employee handbook that relates to policies that cover terms of employment and actions of employees. It is important to review all of these policies and procedures annually. Carefully examine them for potentially discriminatory language and actions that are prohibited by the ADA. Programs may need to add policies that specifically address how the needs of children with disabilities will be met.

Nondiscrimination Statements

All programs need to have a **nondiscrimination statement** that is welcoming and clear, because it will be part of the materials that are distributed to the public. Following are two examples of nondiscrimination statements. The first is quite general, and it meets the requirements of the ADA.

> The early childhood center accepts all children, parents, and staff regardless of race, religion, creed, gender, or disability.

The second example was developed specifically to address the requirements of the ADA.

> In accordance with the requirements of the titles of the Americans with Disabilities Act of 1990, the early childhood center will not exclude any individual with a disability from the full and equal enjoyment of its services and facilities. The early childhood center will make reasonable modifications in its policies, practices, or procedures when such modifications are necessary to afford its services and facilities to individuals with disabilities, unless the modifications would fundamentally alter the nature of its services.

This second example uses language from the law, specifically mentions individuals with disabilities, and describes how this program will make accommodations on an ongoing, case-by-case basis depending on the needs of the individual.

Other Written Program Materials

Marketing and public relations materials help advertise a program and give it a public face. In addition, newsletters and fact sheets are often distributed to families to provide information about ongoing program activities and early childhood issues. These materials create a written record of your program's philosophy. Make sure that the language is inclusive and is distributed in formats that are accessible to all readers.

Admissions and Enrollment Policies

Statements about who is eligible for the program or whom the program admits must be nondiscriminatory. Even when a program does not intend to discriminate, a policy may be worded in such a way that it may screen out children with disabilities. The following example seeks to describe the children that one program is designed to serve.

> The center accepts children ages 3 months to 6 years. Children must be ready to participate in an age-appropriate curriculum that requires typical developmental skills. Children must be toilet trained by age 2½ to continue to be included in the program.

Compare this with the following statement that specifically welcomes children of diverse abilities.

> The Children's House is a child development center that seeks to provide a caring and supportive learning environment for children ages 3 months to 6 years. The curriculum used promotes the social values of sharing, cooperation, and friendship. All children are helped to develop positive self-concepts and to develop tolerance and understanding for others from different backgrounds. The school admits students of any race, color, differing abilities, national and ethnic origin, gender, or creed. The rights, privileges, programs, and activities are made available to all students and their families. We do not discriminate on the basis of race, color, national and ethnic origin, gender, creed, or disability in the administration of any policies or programs.

The first statement could potentially exclude children who do not meet specific developmental milestones, including those who are not toilet trained by age 2½ because of a disability.

In addition to examining policies concerning eligibility and admissions, programs also need to review the forms for admission and enrollment. When a child has applied for admission, programs may ask for contact and demographic information as well as information about the type of early childhood education program the family desires. At this point in the process, programs should not ask about the presence of a disability or any other special need. This type of information could influence the decision to admit a child and could therefore be potentially discriminatory.

The appropriate time to ask for information about a child's health and development is after admission. Enrollment forms should ask the same information from all families, whether a child has a disability or not. All parents should be asked to provide any information that will help a child's program participation; however, parents are not required to disclose that their child has a disability. Programs are only expected to provide reasonable modifications if this information is provided. If programs communicate that they are welcoming and accepting of children with disabilities, then making requests for accommodations is much less difficult.

Placement

Discussions about which classroom a child will be placed in should be made after that child has been accepted. When a child enrolls in a center, a decision is made about placement. The same placement procedure that is used for all children should be used for a child with a disability, but there may be additional considerations.

Placement decisions are often influenced by the availability of space in a specific classroom, and space is usually linked to chronological age. Programs may assume that children with disabilities should be placed with children at a similar developmental level. Although this decision may seem logical at first, it can present problems. For example, if a 4-year-old boy stays in a toddler classroom because he is not talking, then behavior problems may arise because he is so much larger and stronger than the younger children. In addition, some children do progress very slowly developmentally. If placement is tied to developmental level, then a child with significant delays could stay in the same age grouping for a long time while his or her friends move on each year. Therefore, even though a child with a disability may have skills at an earlier developmental level, he or she should enter and move with the group that is as close to his or her chronological age as possible. The child should continue to move with his or her peer group for several reasons. First, the friendships a child makes are critical to the success of integrated programs. If a child with a disability does not move with his or her group, then he or she will lose those friendships. Second, even though a child may not progress on par with his or her classmates, it is important for the staff to recognize that he or she needs to have the experience of new teachers and new learning opportunities.

Chronological Placement

Chronological placement is not always an easy decision. A frequent concern is toilet training. When a child with a disability who uses diapers is placed in a group that does not have children in diapers, changing facilities may be hard to find, the teacher may not expect to change diapers, and extra staff may be needed. In addition, licensing regulations may require running water and specific changing facilities in classrooms where diapering is the norm. If this hurdle arises, then speak with a representative from your licensing office to discuss the necessary adaptations. Because it is a federal law, the ADA will take precedence over state licensing regulations. In some states, these regulations may not have changed to reflect the requirements of the ADA. The bottom line is that the law and subsequent litigation is quite clear. Programs need to make the necessary changes to accommodate children with disabilities who are not toilet trained at the same time as their peers without disabilities. The following scenario describes one child's enrollment.

• • • Ms. Peters applied to the Sunshine Center for her 3-year-old daughter, Hannah. She provided information about Hannah's age and asked that she attend the class for 3-year-olds that meets three times a week. Space was available in that room, and Hannah was admitted. When Ms. Peters completed the enrollment forms for her daughter, she was asked to provide information about Hannah's developmental milestones, her likes and dislikes, and any special needs she might have. Ms. Peters told Ms. Michael, the director, that Hannah had just started walking and that her balance was unsteady. Ms. Michael was concerned because the 3-year-old children were very active, and she was worried that Hannah might get injured. She thought that the 2-year-old class would be a better place for Hannah, but that class was full. Ms. Michael and Ms. Peters discussed these concerns and decided to try the 3-year-old class for a month. Ms. Michael met with the teacher, and together, they rearranged parts of the classroom to make it easier for Hannah to walk around. Ms. Peters asked Hannah's physical therapist to come to the school and show the teacher how to support Hannah's mobility needs. Hannah visited the school several times before her official start date.

On Hannah's first day, she came for just 1 hour, and her mother stayed with her. On the second day, Ms. Peters introduced Hannah and talked to the class at circle time. She explained that Hannah was born early and, because of that, her walking muscles and her balance were affected. She asked the children if any of them had younger brothers or sisters who were just learning to walk, and she reminded them how easily new walkers can lose their balance. Then, to show the children what Hannah's balance felt like, she asked them to stand up, spin in a circle several times, stop, and lift up one leg. The class thought this was hilarious, and at the same time they got some idea of the problems Hannah had with her balance. Finally, Ms. Peters told them that Hannah loved to sing. Then she and Hannah sang several verses of "There Was an Old Lady Who Swallowed a Fly," and the whole class joined in. After circle time, several children invited Hannah to play.

Dual Placement

There are additional considerations when a child attends both an early childhood special education program and an early childhood program or when a child has a **dual placement.** In some school systems, a child may attend a public special education program and receive before- and after-school care in a different community early childhood center. In this situation, it is very important that there be consistent, open, three-way communication among both programs and the family. Everyone needs to recognize the difficulty and potential stress this dual placement presents for a young child. A child has to make transitions between two programs with two teachers, different children, different curricula, and different rules.

Expulsion and Termination

Policies and procedures manuals should include a clear statement about the reasons for and the process of expulsion and termination. Frequently, children are terminated due to behavior difficulties or difficulties between the program and parents. A program policy that states that expulsion and termination are at the discretion of the program administrator is insufficient. Such a general statement does not describe the process for accommodating a child with a disability. When any child is expelled or terminated from a program, it is important to document the steps taken to address any concerns before reaching the point of termination. For example, a parent handbook can list the actions taken before a child is expelled, such as: 1) director, staff, and parents meet to discuss a behavioral concern, 2) an action plan to manage the behavior is created and agreed to by staff and parent, 3) behavior consultants may be used to support program staff, 4) staff and parents will have frequent communication to evaluate the success of the action plan, and 5) when all efforts to bring about change have been exhausted, parents and the director will meet to determine the next course of action. Programs should document in writing the difficulty that occurred, the actions, and the results of the action taken to address the problem.

Exclusion

The ADA specifies two circumstances under which the exclusion of children with disabilities is allowed.

Fundamental Alteration

The first situation is if the care of a child would *fundamentally alter the nature of the program*. For example, a dance school might require all children to audition as part of the admission process. If a child with a disability applies and is unable to dance, then the school could deny admission to that child because admitting such a child would fundamentally alter the nature of the program.

A second example is not quite as clear cut and has to do with the concept of group versus individual care. Full-day early childhood programs are considered group care. If a child has significant needs that must be met on an individual basis, and must have a personal assistant to provide that care, then this could also be a **fundamental alteration** to the program. It is important to remember that the law requires programs to examine each case on an individual basis. In one situation, the family might provide and pay for the personal assistant, and the child is able to participate in the group with that support. In another case, the family might ask the program to pay for a one-to-one aide, and the child does not participate in the group. In the first case, accepting the individual care would be considered a program accommodation. In the second situation, not only is individual care a concern but also providing and paying for the aide would be very costly for the program and could well constitute an undue burden. More about this topic occurs later in the chapter.

Direct Threat

A second reason that programs may exclude a child is if he or she poses a direct threat to either him- or herself or others. In this rare case, the burden of proof is on the program to fully describe the situation, and this cannot be used as a reason to exclude a child prior to admission. In order for a child to be considered a direct threat, a program has to show

- That it has tried to make changes and accommodations

- That these changes and accommodations were unsuccessful

- That the child is likely to cause or continue to cause significant harm to other children and/or staff

Programs must make the determination of a direct threat on an individual basis after conducting an assessment based on reasonable judgment, current medical evidence, and/or the best available objective evidence. The nature, duration, and severity of the risk must be documented as well as the probability that the potential injury will actually occur. In the case of behavioral issues, programs should document how often the behavior in question occurs, the circumstances under which it occurs, and the steps taken by the staff to change the behavior. In addition, the program must indicate what accommodations were used to try to mitigate the risk. These efforts should include written documentation about any communication between the parents and the program staff, any specific program changes, and the results of such efforts. The process for determining direct threat is very similar to the steps taken before expulsion and termination described previously. In this case, all efforts have failed to keep the child, other children, and staff safe from harm. The documentation collected during this process may be used as evidence if the determination of direct threat is challenged.

Undue Burden

Finally, programs do not have to make changes that are very costly. This would constitute an undue burden. If the accommodations needed for a child with a disability are very costly and less expensive alternatives are not found, then centers are not obligated to make the changes. Larger programs with greater financial resources can afford to make more costly changes than smaller programs. A small program would probably not be expected to make costly changes, such as hiring an additional assistant to shadow a child. Again, each request for accommodation must be reviewed on a case-by-case basis.

If the program determines that the accommodations a child needs are too costly and constitute an undue burden, then the director should meet with the parents to discuss alternatives. Parents can decide that they want their child to attend even though certain accommodations cannot be made. They may also decide to withdraw their child because the program cannot meet his or her needs. This decision rests with the family, and the program should not use its inability to make certain changes as a reason to exclude or terminate a child.

Separate Programs

Early childhood programs cannot refuse admission to a child with a disability simply because programs specifically for children with disabilities exist in their community. For example, if a child with Down syndrome applies to a program, then the child cannot be denied admission because another program with services specifically for children with Down syndrome exists in the community. Even if the director believes that the other program might better meet the child's needs, this is not grounds for exclusion or termination. The only exception to this prohibition is if auxiliary aids and services are provided for a specific situation. For example, if a program sponsors several performances of a puppet show, but hires a sign language interpreter for only one performance, then individuals with disabilities needing this service can be encouraged to attend that specific performance.

Other Concerns

All directors confront situations in which a child is unhappy or does not appear to be benefiting from the program for an unknown reason. If this occurs, and the child in question has a disability, then the situation should be handled the same way the program deals with all children. A good first step is to meet with the parents and develop a plan to try and help the child. If concerns persist, then the decision about withdrawal should rest with the parents. An example follows.

• • • Mario attends the 4-year-old class and rarely interacts with the other children in his group. He is not disruptive, but he rarely participates in any of the planned group activities. During circle time, he sits quietly and hums to himself. On the playground, he runs back and forth along the fence. His teacher, Miss Deborah, feels Mario would learn more in a program specifically for children with special needs. She meets with his parents and expresses her concerns. Mario's parents explain that he receives private therapy services, and they want him in the 4-year-old class for the social experience. Even though he keeps to himself, they feel he is benefiting. Under these circumstances, even though Miss Deborah disagrees, there are not grounds for termination under the ADA.

Reasonable Modifications

According to the ADA, early childhood programs are required to make "reasonable modifications in policies, practices, or procedures when such modifications are necessary to afford such goods, services, facilities, privileges, advantages, or accommodations to individuals with disabilities" (42 U.S.C. § 12182 [b][2][A][ii]). These modifications must be readily achievable (i.e., able to be made without undue hardship and expense). The accommodations under this part of the law are the most difficult to determine because they are not clearly defined and can encompass a range of possibilities. In early childhood programs, administrators must think in terms of the developmental program that is provided and any of the caregiving routines needed for young children. The child's program includes the curriculum, schedules, routines, and activities as well as any caregiving routines, such as toileting, personal hygiene, snack, meals, and health care.

The information gathered through the enrollment process should help identify any needed accommodations. Parents can supply valuable information and, in certain situations, provide training about their child's needs and how they should be handled. Administrators can help by supplying information about the program curriculum, schedule, and routines. Information from both parents and administrators can then be combined in a feasible manner to accommodate the needs of the child. Such collaboration serves to meet both the needs of the child with a disability and the smooth operation of an early childhood program. For example, if a child needs a nebulizer treatment before his nap, then a staff member could start the treatment and provide a book for the child to look at near the lunch area. The teacher can monitor the treatment while cleaning up for lunch and setting up the rest area. The child's family needs to indicate how often the treatment needs to be done and needs to train staff to provide the treatment. The administrator and teacher need to write a policy covering medication administration, identify how the procedure will fit into the schedule, identify staff to be trained to carry out the procedure, and document all aspects of the procedure. Both parties need to be sensitive to how incorporating this procedure will feel to the child and how it will appear to the other children and families. Chapter 5 covers program components and discusses specific accommodations that need to be made in the classroom related to curriculum, routines, and activities.

Full Participation

Under the ADA, early childhood programs must include children with disabilities in all activities. This means that creating a separate classroom for children with disabilities is prohibited. Placing all of the children with disabilities in a program in one classroom would not be considered appropriate. Programs must make provisions to ensure that children with disabilities can participate as much as possible in all program activities, including field trips, special activities, and the playground. **Full participation** for children with disabilities requires the resourcefulness and creativity of everyone involved.

Auxiliary Aids and Services

Auxiliary aids and services are the accommodations people with speech-language, learning, hearing, or visual impairments need to communicate effectively. These accommodations might include assistive listening devices, the use of sign language or sign language interpreters, large-print written materials, and braille. Programs must provide auxiliary aids and services unless doing so would fundamentally alter the nature of their program or would impose an undue burden. Centers do not have to incur significant difficulty or expense. The undue burden standard that applies to the provision of auxiliary aids and services, however, requires a greater level of effort than does the readily achievable standard for removing physical barriers in existing facilities described in the next section. Even though the standards are different, the factors to be considered in determining what qualifies as an undue burden are identical to those listed previously for determining what is readily achievable.

Pictures for communication or sign language are two of the most frequently used auxiliary aids used in early childhood programs. A child may have cards or a board with cards that indicate simple items or classroom routines for making choices. There may be a simple sign vocabulary that a child is using. Staff development training can assist the teacher in understanding how to use the communication devices and to learn sign language. If speech-language pathologists (SLPs) are available, then they can provide helpful consultation for the classroom. The teacher and child's classmates can use the cards and signs to help understand what item a child wants or what activity the child wants to do.

The child's parents or caregivers and program staff need to work together to select the optimal method of communication and determine any need for auxiliary aids and services. If a child is deaf and communicates using sign language, then the child's teacher may wish to take a sign language course. When field trips and special programs are arranged, it would be important to ask if a sign language interpreter is available or seek a volunteer who signs to accompany the group. There may be a need for pictures in addition to verbal explanations.

The ADA requires that early childhood programs also have the capacity to communicate with parents who need auxiliary aids and services. Accommodations must also be provided when a parent has a visual or hearing impairment. For example, if a parent is visually impaired, then he or she and the center may agree that all announcements will be read to him or her when she picks up his or her daughter or the message transmitted via his or her voicemail. If a center needs to communicate with parents who are hearing impaired, then the administrator should investigate using a relay service for the hearing impaired provided by the local telephone service. With a relay service, the caller dials a special operator who then transmits the message to or from the person with the hearing impairment. Every state now has a free relay service. An alternative would be to purchase a special telecommunications device (telecommunications device for the deaf or TDD). A TDD sends and receives messages in print when attached to a telephone line.

The law does not require that the program provide services of a personal nature. A program would not be required to provide eyeglasses, hearing aids, or communication devices that are the personal possessions of a child.

Physical Accessibility

Any program administrator can complete a physical accessibility checklist of the program. The ADA web site provides a checklist that can be used to determine if parking lots, entrances, hallways, bathrooms, and classrooms are physically accessibility. Besides the checklist, a tape measure and fish or luggage scale (used to measure the force needed to open a door in pounds) are needed. If any building renovations or new construction are planned, then using this guide will be helpful in determining the changes that must be made in those areas. Another helpful way of determining accessibility is to solicit the assistance of someone who uses a wheelchair, is visually impaired, or is hearing impaired. If individuals with disabilities are not available, then the administrator can use an empty wheelchair or a large stroller to help determine whether spaces have enough turning space and are wide enough.

Once the physical accessibility checklist is completed, it would be appropriate to determine areas that need change and create an action plan with a time line to complete the needed changes. Regardless of whether a program currently includes children who need physical accessibility, consideration should be given to completing no or low-cost changes immediately.

Removing Physical Barriers

The requirements for change are closely tied to the resources of the individual center and will vary from center to center. Centers must assess each potential change or modification and decide on a case-by-case basis which changes can be made. The standard in the law for deciding what centers are required to do to make their facilities physically accessible is the term *readily achievable*, or "easily accomplishable and able to be carried out without much difficulty or expense" (42 U.S.C. 12181 [9]). Centers must remove physical barriers and make architectural changes that can be carried out without much difficulty or expense. Each center must look at the changes required and make these decisions on a case-by-case basis. Changes that are readily achievable for a large corporate child care center might be unrealistic for a small neighborhood program.

If you are hiring a contractor to make small changes, such as building a ramp or retrofitting a bathroom, make sure he or she is fully aware of the accessibility requirements of the ADA. Administrators have added ramps only to find that they are too steep or they do not have enough turning space on landings. In bathrooms grab bars, towel dispensers and sinks have specific installation heights to accommodate individuals using wheelchairs.

Changes do not always have to be expensive. Tables and chairs are movable so that aisles allow the passage of a wheelchair. Most tables in early childhood classrooms have adjustable legs so that a table can be raised to accommodate a wheelchair. Examples of simple, low-cost changes include

- Screening off part of a bathroom to provide privacy for the diapering of older children

- Lowering coat hooks for a child in a wheelchair

- Using labels that can be identified by touch, so a child with a visual impairment can use materials independently

- Adding a light as well as a bell that signals the change in activities

Alternatives to Barrier Removal

If it is not possible to remove a barrier, then programs must investigate other ways to make their facility accessible. If a classroom for 4-year-olds is on the second floor and is to include a child who uses a wheelchair, then consideration should be given to changing the classroom location to the first floor. Similarly, if the bathroom in the classroom is not wheelchair accessible, but there is another classroom with a larger bathroom, then relocating the class could be another option.

An important point to keep in mind is that the needs of children change during the year, and early childhood centers need to continually assess the changes they can make to become and stay as physically accessible as possible without being cost prohibitive. No center is required to exceed the requirements of the law, but centers are required to continue to make efforts to comply with the legal standards.

Transportation

If an early childhood program provides transportation, then it must be physically accessible to all children and the same level of transportation must be offered to all children. If the center offers daily transportation to and from home, then it must offer this service to any child with a disability. Transportation may need to be modified by using a special car seat, removing a seat in a van, and adding "tie-downs" to accommodate a wheelchair.

The transportation standard in the law is the same as that for barrier removal in existing facilities. Early childhood programs must remove transportation barriers to the extent that it is *readily achievable*. For the most part, programs are not required to buy new vehicles or install lifts, but they must remove whatever barriers they can so that transportation is accessible. The major exception is if a center provides regular transportation in vehicles that hold 16 or more people. In this case, vehicles purchased or leased after August 26, 1990, must be modified so that they are readily accessible and usable by people with disabilities. If a program does not regularly provide transportation, but goes on field trips with parent drivers, then the program must make efforts to provide appropriate transportation so a child with disabilities can participate.

Summary

This chapter highlighted many program changes that have been identified through litigation that are issues for early childhood programs. The next chapter will identify a process that an administrator can use to identify areas that need change within the program they supervise.

5

Review for Program Change

Key Concepts: accommodation plan; program review

It is your leadership as an administrator that will bring about the changes for a high-quality, inclusive early childhood program. You have a working knowledge of the ADA and related litigation. The prospect of making program changes may be a bit overwhelming, but if change is approached in a systematic way, then the reward is improvements in the program. As suggested before, if sufficient resources and time are available, then conducting a **program review** is the most thorough and efficient approach. This form of self-study reviews all aspects of your program, including policies and procedures, reasonable modifications to classroom programming, auxiliary aids and services, and physical accessibility. In conjunction with those changes, the need for accompanying staff development and outside resources must be assessed. The information collected in the self-study can be used to develop an **accommodation plan** that will guide future changes. A comprehensive program review may be beyond the manpower and time that your program can afford. Even though this process is not feasible for some centers, any administrator can use this systematic approach to think about what can be done. Planning changes to comply with the law and improve quality is essentially a think, plan, do, and review process. This extensive process is outlined next. Choose the parts that are within your program's capabilities and make a start.

Complete a Program Review

As you begin to think about what changes you may need to make to your program, it is often hard to decide where to start. The following suggestions can help you organize your efforts. You need to make sure that you have identified the topics for your program review and gathered complete information from the program review. To comply with the ADA, a center should have nondiscriminatory admission policies and eligibility criteria for admission, make or prepare to make reasonable modifications to the program so that it is available to children with disabilities and their families, prepare to use auxiliary aids and services, and make the program physically accessible. To comply with the spirit of the law, it is important that all staff understand the law and develop some awareness about disabilities. It is also important for a center to identify resources in the community that can help provide staff training, information, and technical assistance about people with disabilities and the ADA. The areas of compliance as well as staff development and community resources should be the minimum dimensions included in the program review. You should review each of these program aspects thoroughly. Other topics specific to your program should be added at your discretion. Conducting a program review will help you decide what changes your program needs to make. The following steps describe the self-study process and lead you through the development of an accommodation plan.

Assess the Need for Changes in Policies and Procedures

An important first step is to gather all written documents that exist that can help you in the review process. Collect your policies and procedures, operating procedures, parent handbook, admission and enrollment forms, medical forms, brochures, program information, advertising, and so forth. Review all of the documents, note if policies are missing and need to be drafted, and note which documents need revision or replacement.

Policies and procedures are essential to the operation of any good organization. They guide the accomplishment of the mission and goals of the organization. They also ensure that the organization is in compliance with accepted legal standards. Policies and procedures should be written as clearly, completely, and concisely as possible while still addressing the organization's key operations. The basis of policies and procedures are the 1) mission statement and philosophy for your program; 2) all pertinent regulations, such as licensing requirements; and 3) the procedures established to accomplish your mission and meet licensing standards. An operations manual may contain but not be limited to

- Employee policies and procedures
    - Personnel
    - Hiring and recruitment
    - Benefits
    - Training/staff development
    - Evaluation/performance appraisal
    - Termination and grievances
    - Job descriptions
- Financial policies and procedures
    - Budget
    - Tuition
    - Income sources and billing
    - Financial aid/scholarships
- Program policies and procedures
    - Organizational chart
    - Nondiscrimination
    - Admission, program eligibility, discharge
    - Suspected abuse and neglect
    - Health (e.g., medications, injuries, communicable diseases)
    - Discipline and behavior management
    - Records and confidentiality
    - Emergency plans (e.g., program closing, inclement weather, building evacuation)
    - Food service/nutrition
    - Parent involvement
    - Curriculum/educational philosophy
    - Problem resolution/grievances
    - Transportation

There are also other operating procedures that are the "nitty-gritty" of the daily program, help the day flow well, and are more easily subject to change (e.g., taking field trips, volunteering in a classroom, planning birthday and holiday parties).

All formal, written policies of the program need not be included in the consumer information. An informational and more user-friendly version can be adopted. Many centers also have parent handbooks that contain information about the daily operations of the program. It is helpful for prospective parents and parents of children enrolled in the center to know what the programming and policies of a center are like. Topics in a parent handbook may include, but not be limited to

- Purpose and organization of the program
    - History
    - Philosophy/mission statement
    - Nondiscrimination statement
    - Program description/goals
    - Group size and ratios
    - Organizational chart/administrative structure
    - Funding
    - Licensing
- Daily operations
    - Calendar
    - Hours of operation
    - Pick-up and drop-off
    - Absences
    - Parties/graduation
    - Classroom rules
    - Field trips
    - Toilet training
    - Naptime
    - Mealtime
    - What your child should bring to school

- Parent involvement
    - Communication
    - Parent orientation
    - Parent conferences
    - Parent workshops
- Policies and procedures
    - Admissions and withdrawal
    - Eligibility
    - Enrollment
    - Placement
    - Suspension, withdrawal, termination
    - Tuition and other charges
    - Health, illness, injuries, medicine
    - Emergencies
    - Discipline
    - Records and confidentiality

For the policy section of the self-study, you should review all your written program materials, including policies and procedures, brochures/ program information, parent handbook, operating procedures, forms, job descriptions, and so forth. If there are aspects of your program that are not documented in writing, then make notations and start drafting procedures. Carefully review your admission policy to ensure that it is nondiscriminatory and does not screen out or exclude children with disabilities. The information contained in the handbook should also clearly convey the idea that your program does not discriminate against children with disabilities. Table 5.1 shows an example of a self-study checklist for addressing policies and procedures.

Assess the Need for Reasonable Modifications in Programming

The administrator needs to look at various aspects of programming to determine the need for reasonable modifications.

Table 5.1. Self-study checklist addressing policies and procedures

Area	Time line/ review date	Person responsible	Changes needed
Policies and procedures ❏ Brochure/ program information ❏ Parent information ❏ Operating procedures ❏ Forms ❏ Other written materials	Begin as soon as possible; complete review within 3 months; review annually with program evaluation	Committee: program director, parent, and staff member	Policies and procedures complete; reviewed for contradictions to ADA; change policy on toilet training Write and add nondiscrimination statement to program information

Classrooms

The specific changes you make in your classrooms will depend on the needs of the families and children with disabilities in your program. Interview classroom staff members who have had previous experience working with children with disabilities and listen to their suggestions. Try to visit programs that include children with disabilities, such as a preschool special education program and an inclusive community program. Talk to the staff in those programs and get their suggestions and then develop some preliminary ideas about ways to accommodate children with a variety of disabilities in each classroom. Think about the materials and equipment in your classrooms. There should be a variety of learning opportunities that appeal to all of the senses. The curriculum you use should allow for flexibility to meet a variety of group learning needs as well as individualized teaching strategies. The schedule should be predictable with little "down" or waiting time. The blocks of time should be developmentally appropriate for the group. The classroom schedule should be flexible enough to accommodate programming changes.

If children with visual impairments are present, then large items and furniture should remain in place. When items need to be moved, the child with visual impairments should be introduced to the changes. When children are cued to changes in activities using the lights, bells, or verbal directions, all children should be able to discern the cues.

Special activities, such as field trips, may require special planning. As for any classroom activities, the special activity should be available to all children. Planning may include inquiring about accessibility of the transportation for the trip and accessibility of the activities during the trip. Table 5.2 shows an example of a self-study checklist for reasonable modifications in programming.

Table 5.2. Self-study checklist for reasonable modifications in programming

Area	Time line/review date	Person responsible	Changes needed
Reasonable modifications in programming	Begin as soon as possible; finish in 8 weeks; review with each program evaluation	Teacher and assistant; will call and visit early intervention programs, too	Schedules can be adjusted by teachers
Classroom			Curriculum has multilevel adaptations
❑ Schedule			
❑ Curriculum			Room arrangement can be changed to suit needs of students; some rooms very small
❑ Room arrangement			
❑ Equipment/materials			Need toys with more tactile and auditory appeal; get books showing disabilities; find someone who can adapt toys; early intervention staff says to call them with questions
❑ Placement/promotion			All children *must* move each year to next group; review this policy

Table 5.3.   Self-study checklist for auxiliary aids and services

Area	Time line/ review date	Person responsible	Changes needed
Auxiliary aids and services	Begin as soon as possible; finish in 2 weeks; review with program evaluation	Program director	No students in need of adaptations, aids, or services now; have called telephone company for information for future; one parent, visually impaired, has made arrangements to call another parent who will read all written materials

Assess the Need for Auxiliary Aids and Services

People with hearing, visual, learning, or speech-language impairments may need accommodations or auxiliary aids and services to enable them to communicate effectively. For example, someone who is hearing impaired, but lip reads, may need to be accommodated by sitting close enough to see the speaker. Ensuring effective communication may also require the use of auxiliary aids and services, such as sign language interpreters, notetakers, large-print written materials, and assistive listening devices. Think about some possible alternatives to written and spoken communication that children might use. Table 5.3 shows an example of a self-study checklist for auxiliary aids and services.

Assess the Physical Accessibility

A copy of the ADAAG is available from the Architectural and Transportation Compliance Board or from the U.S. Department of Justice web site. The ADAAG contains all of the required measurements for physical accessibility and provides the standards for remodeling of current facilities and construction of new facilities. The guidelines will help you evaluate your existing building. Use the checklist in Appendix D in the back of the book for play area standards.

Assessing the physical accessibility of your program will take time. You may wish to hire a consultant, such as an architect or someone with experience in universal design. The Architecture and Transportation Compliance Board and the regional Technical Assistance Center of the

Table 5.4. Self-study checklist of physical accessibility

Area	Time line/review date	Person responsible	Changes needed
Entrances; hallways; stairways	Begin as soon as possible; complete in 6 weeks	Consultant; program director	Check incline of ramp at entrance
Other access to goods and services (classrooms, play spaces, cafeteria, meeting rooms, playground, staff lounge, offices)	Begin as soon as possible; complete in 4 weeks	Program director; classroom staff	Furniture needs to be re-arranged to allow wider aisles
Access to restrooms			Meets guidelines
Other necessary measures	Investigate as soon as possible	Program director	No accessible signage
Play areas	Investigate as soon as possible	Consultant; program director; board	Needs soft surface; wood chips not sufficient
Transportation: parking and sidewalks	Begin as soon as possible; finish in 4 weeks; review with program evaluation	Program director; consultant	No transportation provided; parents agree to transport for field trips Disability parking space by door designated and marked; assess how many spaces are needed Sidewalks okay; need curb cut from parking lot

National Institute on Disability and Rehabilitation Research are good resources. With your copy of the checklist, a clipboard, pencils, and a flexible steel tape measure, look at each program space from the perspective of someone with mobility difficulties who may need special support to walk or may be using a wheelchair. The checklist guides you through parking areas, entrances, hallways, bathrooms, and classroom spaces. For example, there should be adequate space for a person using a wheelchair to turn around and get through walkways, doorways, and paths. Sinks or table surfaces should be high enough for a wheelchair to slide under. Next, assess each space from the perspective of a person with a sensory impairment. There should be visual, tactile, or auditory cues for individuals who are deaf, hard of hearing, or visually impaired. Walk or move through each space in the facility to assess it. Use the accessibility checklist (see Table 5.4) to make sure that you have completed a thorough study of the physical environment. Note areas that need improvement and record your findings.

Transportation should also be assessed for accessibility (see Table 5.5). There should be a clearly designated parking space or spaces close to entrances for an individual with mobility difficulty. The vehicle seats should accommodate a child with poor sitting balance. The vehicle should have the appropriate attachments if wheelchairs are transported. Again, refer to the ADAAG standards to guide your study.

Assess the Need for Staff Development

Survey your staff to find out what training and experience they have had related to people with disabilities. Ask what information and support they would like in order to feel more comfortable and knowledgeable. Ask what their concerns and hopes are for this new experience. Make sure that these are addressed when you develop a training plan. Table 5.6 on page 61 shows an example of a self-study checklist for addressing staff development needs, and Table 5.7 on page 61 shows a sample staff training plan.

Table 5.5. Self-study checklist for transportation

Area	Time line/ review date	Person responsible	Changes needed
Lift for wheel-chairs Tie-downs for wheelchairs Car seats	Implement now; review annually	Consultant; representative from The Arc of the United States	Get estimate on retrofitting current van; purchase portable ramp; remove seats; install tie-downs

Table 5.6.   Self-study checklist for addressing staff development needs

Area	Time line/ review date	Person responsible	Changes needed
Staff training ❏ Knowledge ❏ Needs ❏ Training plan	As soon as possible; finish in 1 week; review annually	Program director	Add section on working with children with disabilities to the current needs assessment for training; administer to staff; develop training plan based on findings

Table 5.7.   Staff training plan

Date	Topic/content	Time
September	**Values and attitudes about disabilities** Speaker from disabilities advocacy group	2 hours
November	**Disability awareness** Speaker from The Arc of the United States	1 hour
January	**Inclusion philosophy** Panel of parents, representatives from special education program, teacher of a child with disabilities	2 hours
March	**Understanding special education** Speakers from the public school system	2 hours
May	**Strategies for successful inclusion** Private educational consultant	2 hours
Total		9 hours

Table 5.8.   Self-study checklist addressing disability resources

Area	Time line/ review date	Person responsible	Changes needed
Resources ❏ Disability resources ❏ Americans with Disabilities Act resources	Begin as soon as possible; ongoing	Program director, with help of staff and parents	Program has current listing of resources; add section on disability-related topics; find out if information can be stored on the computer; develop system to add new resources

Assess the Need for Resources

Collect information about national, state, and local agencies that can offer you advice, information, and technical assistance on the laws and specific disabilities (see Appendix B in the back of this book). The ADA expects programs to aggressively seek out resources to help with the changes needed to include children, families, and employees with disabilities (see Table 5.8). Having this listing in advance will be a great benefit when and if you need to use it. Your listing might include the following information:

• Agency name

• Name of contact person

• Address

• Telephone and fax number

• Services provided

After completing a thorough program review, you will have enough data to begin creating a plan to address the identified areas that need changes.

6

The Accommodation
Plan and Implementation

> **Key Concepts:** confidentiality; nondiscrimination
> policy

After you have completed your program review, it is best to have a systematic way to organize the data you collected and address the areas that need changes. One way to do this is to create an accommodation plan. The following steps will guide you through that process.

Convene an Americans with Disabilities Act Work Group

The purpose of an ADA work group is to review the information from your program review and develop a plan that identifies changes that are needed, examines how changes can be made, and monitors progress toward completing the changes. The group members should include at least a teacher, a parent, and an administrator. It is also important to invite a person who has a disability, someone who represents an advocacy organization for people with disabilities, or a parent of a child with a disability. A person with disability-related experience will be able to look at your program and help you identify changes that might otherwise be overlooked. Define with the group the goals of the program review, the length and extent of the time commitment, and how tasks will be completed and documented.

Convening a work group may not be feasible. You may complete the program review and create an accommodation plan by yourself. Try to develop a way to have outside people review your plan and give you some objective criticism. You may have an administrators' group that meets to discuss professional issues. See if someone from the group will talk to you about your plan. There may be an individual with a disability or someone from a disability advocacy group that would discuss your plan with you.

Establish a Time Line

The work group needs to develop a realistic schedule for reviewing the information from the program review and develop an accommodation plan to implement the proposed changes. Set a deadline for completion of the work.

Develop a Nondiscrimination Policy

The discussion of a nondiscrimination statement occurred in the previous chapter. This statement reflects your program's commitment to the spirit of the ADA. Any new written policy should be reviewed by the appropriate governing board of your program. Most programs already have a philosophy, mission statement, or program description that will need only simple revisions. Chapter 4 contained an example of a program philosophy that included a statement of nondiscrimination with reference to including individuals with disabilities.

Summarize the Problems and Solutions

After you finish the self-study, summarize and record the results. Figure 6.1 is one example of how to organize the information into an accommodation plan. Include notations of problems and propose solutions. First, consider solutions that would not have an impact on the budget (i.e., no-cost solutions). For example, ask local community agencies if they can provide volunteers for the classrooms. A local university or community college may be able to provide speakers for your staff development programs. Although there are time, effort, and planning costs on the part of the children, families, and staff, many creative solutions will have little budget impact. Next, organize other solutions into low-cost and high-cost categories.

Common Problems and Solutions for Compliance

The next sections give examples of some common problems and a variety of solutions to be used in the compliance plan. The format of the accommodation plan parallels the format of the self-study.

Area	Fully met (comments)	Partially met		Not met	
		Problems	Solutions	Problems	Solutions
Policies and procedures					
a. Brochure/program information					
b. Parent information					
c. Forms					
d. Other written materials					
Reasonable program modifications					
1. Classroom					
a. Schedule					
b. Curriculum					
c. Room arrangement					
d. Equipment/materials					
e. Placement/promotion					
2. Transportation					
a. Vehicles					
b. Parking					
c. Sidewalks					
3. Auxiliary aids and services					
4. Physical accessibility					
a. Entrances, hallways, and stairways					
b. Other access to goods and services (e.g., classrooms, play spaces, cafeteria, meeting rooms, playground, staff lounge, offices)					
c. Access to restrooms					
d. Other necessary measures					
5. Staff awareness and training					
1. Knowledge					
2. Needs					
3. Training plan					
6. Resources					
1. Disability resources					
2. ADA resources					

Figure 6.1 Accommodation plan.

Policies and Procedures

Issue: Your program policies and procedures need revision to comply with the ADA.

No-cost solution: Adopt materials that have already been developed and are in compliance with the ADA, such as waivers from settlements of ADA cases.

Low-cost solutions: Write up amendments and add them to current materials.

High-cost solutions: Rewrite and publish all program materials to reflect any changes in philosophy.

Physical Accessibility Problems

Issue: The program has classrooms on two floors with a standard stairway.

No-cost solution: Move the classroom of a child with physical disabilities from the second floor to a ground level room so it is accessible.

Low-cost solution: If practical, obtain a portable, folding ramp that can be transported and used in many places.

High-cost solution: Consult with building contractors and equipment suppliers to estimate costs of proposed modifications, such as building ramps or widening doorways. Sometimes physical alteration is the only acceptable solution. (Remember that any new construction must meet ADA accessibility guidelines before it is built.)

Reasonable Modifications Issues

Each program is required to make reasonable modifications in policies, practices, or procedures. Examples of changes to classroom activities, transportation, and resources are described.

Classroom

Issue: A young child is not as independent as his peers and wanders out of the classroom.

No-cost solutions: Talk to other teachers about older students who could assist as tutors in activities that are difficult for this child. Try to locate classroom volunteers to assist all the students.

Low-cost solutions: Ask if a simple latch can be installed out of the children's reach. Look for special education consultants in your community who would be available for assistance when the need arises to make changes in your programming.

High-cost solution: Hire a teaching assistant to help all of the children, so the child who wanders can be watched easily.

Transportation

Issue: Transportation for a child with a disability is needed.

No-cost solution: Family or employee voluntarily provides own transportation.

Low-cost solutions: See if there are volunteer organizations in your community who can assist with transportation. See if the child in need of transportation is entitled to transportation or assistance with the cost of transportation as part of their personal benefits. Adapt an existing van by buying a portable ramp, removing a seat, and installing a wheelchair tie-down.

High-cost solutions: Buy a van with lift. Make arrangements for hiring special transportation.

Auxiliary Aids and Services

Issue: A child is hearing impaired and uses a hearing aid. The parents are also hearing impaired.

No-cost solution: Have parents provide information and teach staff how to insert hearing aids and test battery for their child.

Low-cost solutions: Locate professionals in your community who are available for sign interpretation. Investigate the cost of a relay service through your local telephone company.

High-cost solutions: Purchase a TDD.

Staff Training

Issue: Staff request information about the ADA and inclusion.

No-cost solutions: Locate local resources that can provide in-service training at no cost. Therapists and parents of children with disabilities are often willing to help train staff. Universities and community colleges may be good sources of instructors.

Low-cost solutions: Write a grant to support training for your staff. Find local funding for in-service training.

High-cost solutions: Hire consultants to provide training. Budget money to support staff development provided at local colleges, universities, and professional conferences.

Resources

Issue: You need to find people to answer questions about the ADA and provide guidance and information about the laws regarding including a child with disabilities.

No-cost solution: Staff and parents search for local resources to support children with disabilities.

Low-cost solution: Purchase materials and resources that provide information about supporting children with disabilities.

High-cost solution: Allocate money in the budget to hire consultants to advise about including children with disabilities.

This is only a sample of issues and potential solutions. Administrators should try to network with other program administrators who have similar concerns. Inquire at professional meetings how other centers are making program accommodations. Talk to staff, parents, and governing boards to brainstorm solutions to problem areas. Seek the help of the Child Care Law Center and the ADA technical assistance center in your region.

Set Priorities for Making Changes

If you need help understanding federal, state, or local requirements, contact your regional ADA technical assistance center. Written materials, such as policies and procedures, program descriptions, brochures, parent handbooks, and staff training, are usually revised regularly, so you can incorporate needed revisions about serving children with disabilities during that process. You should consider a range of program changes and accommodations that might be needed if and when a child with disabilities is enrolled. Think of possible situations and develop a process you can use to make the modifications. Be ready to make necessary changes as the need arises. Decide which solutions best address the identified problems. Prioritize the list of solutions and make a schedule for completing the changes. Designate the person responsible for each task.

Complete the Options that Have Little or No Cost

The options that have little or no cost may seem the simplest solutions to implement. It is still important, however, to assign these tasks and follow up on their completion.

Budget for and Make Low-Cost Adaptations and Accommodations

Completing some of the low-cost solutions may require a review of the budget to see if funds are available. It may necessitate reallocating previously designated funds or seeking new money.

Consider and Plan for Alterations, Renovations, and Purchases that Would Involve Greater Cost

High-cost changes will involve seeking new funding, and some of the changes will need to wait until funding can be found. Do not forget to take advantage of any tax credits for which your organization is eligible. Document what you would do if funding were available. Clearly state the changes in which costs exceed the financial capability of your program.

Document Your Efforts

Keep notes from the work group, records of completed work, and plans for program changes for compliance on file. Although the law does not require a self-study and an accommodation plan, you now have written documentation showing that you have given careful consideration to adjusting your program to accommodate children with disabilities.

Implementation

Once you have completed the accommodation plan, it is important to follow through and make the changes required. During the first year, the implementation should be monitored frequently to document progress and make revisions if new barriers are encountered. Circumstances may arise that necessitate new considerations or revisions to plans that are already made. After the accommodation plan has been completed, review it annually to reevaluate whether more or different improvements are readily achievable. Examine the changes that you have made in the past year in each of the self-study areas, and see if additional ones are needed. Add your ADA accommodation plan to your program evaluation, and update it on a regular basis.

Although the program change process outlined in the previous chapter may not be feasible for every program, it provides a framework to begin thinking about possible changes and gives some suggestions about how to make changes. It is important to start today to think about how and what might be needed to accommodate the next child seeking admission. Most of these changes are good for all children, not just a child with disabilities.

Financial Assistance for Making Accommodations

Assistance for making changes to comply with the law is available to programs that pay federal income taxes. A tax credit is available to small businesses for expenses incurred for the purpose of making accommodations. A tax deduction is available for qualified architectural and transportation barrier removal expenses. For more information on these tax provisions, contact your local Internal Revenue Service office. Investigate assistance that may be available from state and local governments. A local disability advocacy organization may be able to direct you to other resources for financial assistance and tax benefits.

Insurance

Early childhood facilities may not deny admission to children with disabilities even if admitting children with disabilities results in an increase in insurance premiums or a cancellation of coverage. The ADA is very specific on this point because insurance requirements have frequently been used to exclude people with disabilities from a variety of programs and activities. This issue is difficult because the law does not require insurance companies to provide coverage. If a program is faced with higher rates or cancellation of a policy, then it may eventually have to sue the insurance company to compel the company to prove that its actions are based on sound actuarial data. In other words, insurance companies must base their rates on objective information. They must have evidence that a person with a disability is a greater insurance risk in order to raise their rates or cancel the policy. If your insurance company raises your rates, then you should request that it provide you with information supporting its position that there is indeed a greater risk or likelihood of increased risk in serving children with disabilities. An insurance company does not have to tell the business it is insuring how the rates are established. If it appears that a particular insurance company has a common practice of discrimination, then try contacting your state commissioner of insurance. As increasing numbers of programs are faced with this untenable situation, this area of the law may be the subject of litigation that will prompt change.

Parents with Disabilities

Communication with parents is an integral part of early childhood programs. The ADA also applies to parents or caregivers who have disabilities. You are responsible for ensuring that parents and family members have full access to your center. In addition to physical accessibility, this may mean adapting the way you communicate with families to meet the needs of someone with a visual or hearing impairment. Such accommodations do not have to be expensive. Reading parent notices and newsletters is an alternative to having them available in braille. The best strategy for providing accommodations is to ask the person directly how best to meet his or her needs.

Confidentiality

An administrator must create and enforce a strict policy of maintaining **confidentiality** about personal information of all children and families participating in the program. All staff should be reminded that no one should discuss child and family information outside of appropriate program discussions, such as staff meetings about a child's development. Questions may be asked about the child with a disability when family members notice the differences in children. Although assuring the family of the child with a disability that no information is shared without permission, it is appropriate to ask the family how they would like questions that arise to be handled.

Summary

You now have a process to assess your program and create a plan to address changes needed to better include young children with disabilities. The next section will move from the broad program issues to more specific strategies for working with staff, parents, and children.

III

Program Components

This section provides guidance on communicating with staff, families, and children about what the law requires and how it will affect them. The section on staff communication discusses issues related to interviewing and orientation, concerns and fears about inclusion, development of a learning plan, and supportive supervision. The section on communicating with families provides information about establishing a positive relationship and addressing concerns about health, safety, and learning. The section also includes information about how children understand disabilities and age-appropriate communication strategies.

The early childhood program administrator plays a key role in determining how staff, children, and families will react to the inclusion of children with disabilities. Research confirms the soundness of this approach. If the administrator communicates a positive attitude and a firm belief that children with and without disabilities benefit from learning and growing together, then it sends a clear message to staff, children, and families.

7

Communicating with Staff

For new staff, the inclusion philosophy needs to be clearly stated during the recruitment and hiring process. Check to see that each job description clearly describes the program's expectations for supporting and teaching all children. Ideally, all applicants will have experience with or a willingness to learn about caring for and teaching children with disabilities. Personal care is part of the job, so essential job functions for all classroom positions will likely include lifting and carrying, feeding, diapering, and toileting.

Modifying Job Descriptions

Job descriptions need to include all the important aspects of the position. The first step is to identify the major responsibilities of the job. What are the key tasks the employee must perform? List each task and estimate the percentage of time spent on each responsibility. This list eventually will become the **essential functions.** Other tasks that are important but not essential may be listed under **nonessential functions.**

Remember to include the physical demands of the job in your list of essential functions. For example, being able to lift and carry children is an important part of a teacher's responsibility in an infant or toddler classroom. Specify how much time the employee is likely to spend performing each physical demand and the approximate weight the employee will be expected to lift. A job description for a teacher in the infant classroom might include frequent lifting and carrying of children weighing approximately 14–30 pounds, but a job description for a substitute teacher who floats among several classrooms might include a weight range of up to 50 pounds to reflect the weight of children ages 2–5.

In addition to the physical demands of the job, consider the mental demands, the general working conditions, the type of communication skills required, and any equipment that must be used. All of these requirements should be included in the job description.

Writing a Job Description

The written job description should give the potential employee a clear idea of the scope of work required. It is not necessary to list all of the specific tasks, but the major responsibilities should be defined clearly. Job descriptions should be updated regularly. It is a good idea to review the description before you advertise an open position. A job description should include the following components:

Title: Use a short, descriptive name for the position.

Qualifications: This section states the minimum knowledge and skill level necessary to perform the job (e.g., education level, number of years of experience). Think about what abilities, skills, and knowledge are important for the prospective employee to possess. Be sure to describe those attributes in this section. The specifications should be consistent with your licensing standards.

Supervision: Provide the title of the supervisor to whom this individual reports.

Objective: This section describes the overall function and responsibilities of the job. It should be no more than one paragraph long and should complement, but not repeat, the job duties section.

Duties: This section states the specific job duties, including the essential and nonessential job functions. List the duties in order of importance and include the percentage of time devoted to each major task. Try to keep the language clear and simple. It helps to begin each sentence with a verb. General nonessential tasks often are covered by including the phrase, "performs all other duties as assigned," at the end of the description.

Existing Staff

If this is the first time that children with disabilities will be included in your program, then teachers will likely have a number of concerns. Introducing the idea of inclusion is a big change and, like any change, will provoke anxiety and resistance. This section describes a process for addressing staff concerns and developing a plan to provide information and support.

For existing staff, including children with disabilities may represent a significant change in their jobs. This may not be what they expected when they were hired. Because the retention of staff is always a concern in the early childhood field, the following strategies may help reassure staff during the change process. As an administrator, your role is to bring your staff together, address their concerns, provide information and ongoing training, and identify community resources to support their efforts.

If you are including children with disabilities for the first time in your program, then a first step might be to schedule several meetings to talk about the changes. These meetings serve two purposes. First, they provide a forum for staff to express concerns. Second, they can lead to creative strategies you can put to use as you begin to look at your program and plan changes to ensure compliance with the ADA. All staff should have genuine input to produce collaborative strategies.

Introducing the Idea of Inclusion

It is important for everyone to understand the requirements of the law and to have the chance to express their concerns and feelings about including children with disabilities. Provide some background on the laws that require early childhood programs to be nondiscriminatory. The information and resources in Section I and in Appendix C at the end of the book can get you started. Keep the information simple for now. You can buy other materials for your resource library that staff and parents can read later for more detail.

Typical Staff Concerns

Many staff concerns spring from negative societal attitudes and values about people with disabilities. Before your staff can welcome children with disabilities into your program, their feelings must be addressed and discussed. By bringing their concerns out in the open, you let people know they are not alone in their doubts. Before you start this process, though, you need to feel comfortable. Talk with other administrators and gather some resources, so you will be prepared to address your teachers' concerns.

One director of a large child care center started her staff meeting by talking about the ADA as an extension of the civil rights protection afforded to many minorities:

"I remember as a child feeling like I just didn't belong. After the first few days of kindergarten, I went home and asked my mother, 'Where do the kids like me go to school?' My father was Indian, and my mother was Latina. All the children I went to school with were Caucasian, and this was the first time I realized I was different."

This story led to a discussion among the staff of many childhood memories of not fitting in and being excluded. By encouraging people to share personal experiences, you can promote an empathetic environment, and staff members can begin to understand how the children in their care may feel.

Another option is to start a discussion with your staff by asking them to remember a time in their childhood when they felt like they did not fit in. Following are some examples of conversation starters:

"I remember being teased when I got glasses in third grade."

"I went to a birthday party in pants only to find all the other girls in party dresses."

Ask your staff members how they feel when they see a person with a disability.

"I was shopping and saw this man in a wheelchair trying to reach the soda. I didn't know what to do. Should I have offered to help, or would that have been rude?"

"On a museum tour, a woman had braces on both legs and walked with crutches. It looked so hard for her to walk up a few steps. I caught myself staring and thinking how lucky I was."

"I was in a fast-food restaurant, and the young woman wiping the tables had a disability. I didn't know people like her could hold a job. It was obvious that she took her responsibilities seriously."

As your staff start to share these experiences, they will find that they are not alone in their fears. They will begin to be more comfortable thinking and talking about children with disabilities.

"When we first started talking about people with disabilities, I was really uncomfortable. But as we talked more, I found out that I wasn't the only one who felt that way. Now that we've had these meetings, I feel closer to my co-workers."

Conversations like these can help staff see that people with disabilities have often been excluded from many things that most people take for granted because of unfounded prejudices. They can begin to understand how much being left out and labeled "different" can hurt.

Developing a Philosophy to Guide Including Children with Disabilities

The next step is to decide what inclusion will look like in your program. Does inclusion mean that any child with a disability could potentially enroll? What about a child with significant disabilities? What classroom should a child attend if he or she is chronologically 3 years old but cannot speak or is not toilet trained? What about a child whose behavior is disruptive? How many children with special needs should be in one class? The following questions can help guide the process of deciding how inclusion will work in your program.

1. What is the role of parents in deciding placement and services?

2. What are the benefits and drawbacks of having children with and without disabilities in the same classroom?

3. What skills and knowledge are necessary to teach children with disabilities versus those needed to teach children without disabilities?

4. What type of classroom support would staff want in order to make inclusion work?

5. What will be the impact on class size and ratios when children with disabilities are part of the group?

These questions can provide a starting point for your discussion. It can be helpful to invite a teacher or administrator from a program that has been successful in including children with disabilities to talk about how these issues have been handled in that program.

The next step is to develop a list of beliefs that everyone feels is central to the mission of providing good care for all children. Programs should have a unified philosophy rather than separate statements for children without disabilities and for children with disabilities. Following are some sample statements:

• We believe that children with and without disabilities are more alike than different.

• We believe that all children have the right to the best possible care and education.

- We believe that all children are different and that those differences should be acknowledged and honored.

- We believe that children with and without disabilities can learn from each other.

This list can then lead to a revised mission statement, such as

> We believe that all children deserve the chance to grow and learn together. Our program provides a safe and nurturing setting that respects the individuality of each child and fosters self-esteem. All children are valued and appreciated for who they are. We help all of the children in our care develop to their full potential.

Addressing Fears and Concerns

It is natural for staff to worry about how inclusion will affect their classrooms and the entire program. Your role, as administrator, is to help your staff feel that they can express themselves freely and that you will hear and respond to their concerns. The following list includes concerns common to many programs:

- Teacher–child ratios

- Sufficient time for each child

- Safety for self and others

- Special equipment

- Fear of hurting the child with a disability

- Lack of knowledge about disabilities

- Uncertainty about how to teach a child with a disability

- Potentially negative reactions of the other children and parents

Think about ways to address these concerns through regular staff development activities. Strategies might include bringing in speakers, visiting other programs, having several workshops, and exploring articles online or in early childhood publications. It is also important to offer to meet privately with any staff person who wants to talk individually. There may be personal concerns that would not come up in a public forum.

Developing a Learning Plan

Building an inclusive program takes time. A good next step is to put your revised mission and philosophy in writing, publish it in your next newsletter, and inform parents and the public about these changes. Consider developing a yearlong **learning plan** to guide the transition toward becoming a more inclusive program. This plan would include strategies for learning more about specific disabilities, special education services, teaching techniques, and program adaptations. One option is to establish committees to manage the work. One committee could coordinate professional development workshops, another could review admissions policies and establish new placement procedures, and a third committee could investigate community resources to support inclusion efforts.

Parents are important allies in this process and provide support as you move toward inclusion. Consider inviting a few parents who have children with disabilities to do a presentation about the family perspective.

As you review your current admissions policies, check again to be sure they comply with the ADA. Do not wait until you are actually receiving a child with a disability. Be prepared and proactive.

There are a number of community resources that can provide ongoing support. Here is a preliminary list of resources to investigate:

1. The special education resources in your public schools

2. The disability organizations in your community, such as The Arc of the United States (formerly the Association for Retarded Citizens), Parents of Down Syndrome (PODS), Easter Seals, Learning Disabilities Association of America (LDA), and United Cerebral Palsy (UCP)

As you plan for the inclusion of children with disabilities in your program, think about your overall program structure and your curriculum. Can your program accommodate the needs of children with widely varying abilities? How can you increase your ability to meet the needs of all the children and at the same time provide support for your staff?

Multi-age Groupings

One solution to accommodating children at different developmental levels is **multi-age groupings.** Instead of having groups of only 2-, 3-, and 4-year-olds, arrange classes with children ranging in age from 2 to 3 or from 2 to 4. In each class, there will be several children in each age range. Montessori classrooms have always had multi-age groupings, often with children from 3 to 5 years in one room. Although your state licensing standards may be written for single-age groups, you can talk with your state or local licensing agency to see if it will permit multi-age groupings and adjust ratio and group size requirements accordingly.

Team Teaching

Team teaching is another creative approach to teaching diverse groups of children. By pairing the 2-year-old class with the 3-year-old class for several activity times throughout the day, you can increase the options for children grouped both chronologically as well as developmentally. The two teachers can offer a variety of activities and the children can choose according to their interest. This way total group size is not increased and the teaching staff can coordinate their efforts.

These combinations allow the children to experience a wide developmental range of activities. Children are free to work on activities that match their developmental needs and interests. They also give the mature 4-year-olds the opportunity to be helpers. Children often do not have a chance to really help, and being a "buddy" can boost the self-esteem and skills of both the "helper" and the "helpee." In addition, this team-teaching approach provides support for the teachers because it gives them a chance to share ideas and discuss problems.

Classroom Teams

Including children with disabilities is a challenge and teachers benefit from the support and shared responsibilities. You can create an important support system for your staff by creating strong classroom teams, establishing specific roles and responsibilities for each team member, and scheduling regular meetings to discuss how the team is working.

If you decide to develop teams, then they should be responsible for deciding how the classroom runs. If you decide to pair two classrooms full time or part time, then the staff from both classrooms would form one team. The team should include the teachers, the teaching assistants, any volunteers, the program director or assistant director, and any specialists or consultants who are working with a child in the room. Other individuals should be invited to participate in team discussions as needed. For example, when the team is planning to discuss changing a child's classroom, the parents should be included in the meeting. Your support staff are valuable team members, too, so remember to include the administrative assistant, bus driver, cook, or custodian as needed.

Four to six people on a team generally works well. Keep the team small, so everyone can contribute. The team still can meet even if one person is absent.

Teams, by definition, need to work closely together. When you begin to think about teams, you may want to ask your staff to identify people with whom they would like to work. Allowing staff to select their teams will contribute to the likelihood of successful team relationships.

Getting Teams Started

Teams should schedule regular times to discuss each child in the room. They should talk about scheduling, placement, classroom activities, and anything else that affects how their room runs. For behavioral and social issues, a mental health consultant can be extremely helpful.

Effective teams do not develop overnight. They need clear goals and rules for functioning. Meet with each team and help the participants think through the guidelines that will work for them.

Each team has to decide how it will make decisions. Some people decide to vote; other people discuss an issue until all participants agree. Basic ground rules help each team's productivity and reduce frustration.

An hour is usually an adequate time for a team meeting. An agenda, developed in advance, can help ensure that all important issues are discussed. Another good tool is to use a notebook placed in the classroom for people to jot down concerns as they arise during the day. These ideas or concerns can become meeting agenda items. Other ideas can be added to the agenda at the beginning of the meeting.

Start each meeting with a brief review of issues that were discussed at the last meeting. Anyone with a pressing problem should be encouraged to talk about it first; then, the team can go on with the planned agenda. At the end of the meeting, summarize the decisions that were made. The summary reminds the team members of the responsibilities they chose and the deadline for their completion. The summary should be circulated right after the meeting. It is a good reminder of what needs to be done, and it is a quick way for people to catch up if they miss a meeting.

Supportive Supervision

People come to you when they need help with a problem. Your supervision and mentorship can provide important support when a staff person is in trouble.

As a supervisor, you can guide your staff through a problem-solving process. You can guide a teacher through an information-gathering process. For example, if a teacher is concerned about a child, then you might want to know if there have been any changes in the child's life, either at home or at school. Is anything different? Is the behavior of concern happening at a specific time or during a certain activity? Is it happening at home, too?

In addition to problem solving, you also provide important emotional support. Teachers need to know that their concerns have been heard and that you will work with them to solve the problem. Here is an example of how a director provided important support.

• • • Denise felt a lot better after talking with her director about a problem she was having with one of her students. Denise had figured out that Leyna, age 2, was pinching other children the first thing in the morning and late in the afternoon. She spoke with Leyna's mother and found out that Leyna's grandmother was very ill, and Leyna's father was away visiting her. There had been quite a lot of turmoil in the family over the past few weeks. Leyna had started pinching her mother and crying when it was time to go to school.

Denise then talked with her director again. They now knew that Leyna was upset and worried. Together they decided to help ease the transition in the morning by arranging for Denise to spend some time reading quietly with Leyna before sending her off to play. In the afternoon, Denise would remind Leyna that Mom would be there soon and give her some extra hugs. The director complimented Denise on her sensitivity and commitment to helping Leyna through this difficult time.

For the next week, the director also checked in with Denise every afternoon. The director continued to provide encouragement as Leyna slowly began to improve. On two afternoons, the director stayed in the classroom to give Denise an extra 10-minute break. By the end of the week, Leyna rarely pinched.

Listening and problem solving are very important supervisory tools, but they are not enough. Your staff need to know that you will act promptly to support them and follow up regularly.

Any changes in your program should be communicated to your families. As you begin to include children with disabilities, it is a good idea to meet with parents to discuss the changes and answer questions.

Changes take time. Preparing to include children with disabilities and providing support to your staff are long-term endeavors. The staff meetings, workshops, and team meetings may require creative scheduling to allot some hours during the workday and some after-work hours for these activities. Look to parents and other volunteers for assistance. Some parents may be willing to help in the classroom, so a team can meet. Using volunteers during naptime can give staff time off during a day when they need to stay late for a workshop.

Even with extra help, these tasks can seem overwhelming. Remember, you do not have to do it all at once. You know your program best. Decide what is most important, and start small. Finally, as an administrator, you need support. Use the formal and informal networks available to you. Talk with other administrators about issues and ideas. Many early childhood programs are facing the same dilemmas. You need regular reminders that you are not alone and that your efforts are for a good cause—quality care and education for all children.

8

Communicating
with Families

> **Key Concept:** inclusion

A comfortable relationship between the family and the early childhood program staff makes it easier for everyone to work together to help a child. Good communication is the key to building such a relationship and is critical when a child has a disability. This relationship may develop without much effort, but at times relationships get off on the wrong foot, as one person's efforts at communication are misunderstood by the other person. Parents may hear only criticism; directors may feel parents are uncooperative. Communication is a two-way street, and both the program and the family can feel frustrated when well-intentioned comments are given unintended meanings. Directors and parents rely on each other for information about how children feel and act both at home and in the program. Open communication can make them strong allies as they work together to nurture and support the children they love.

When a child has a disability, a good relationship between the program and the parent is especially important. The director, the teacher, and the parents need to be able to talk openly about difficult and emotionally painful topics. For parents, talking about their child's disability can remind them of their child's limitations and make them fearful that their child will be treated differently or will be asked to leave the program.

The following comments from teachers and parents reveal the concerns they feel when a child with a disability begins a new program.

"I decided not to tell the preschool that Matthew had cerebral palsy. I didn't want them to treat him any different. I just wanted him to be one of the kids."

87

One mother said,

"I worried every day that the teacher would tell me that Jacob was too much trouble, and he would have to leave the program. It was such a relief to learn that other children had bad days too."

Directors and teachers also may be reluctant to raise potentially difficult topics. They may be afraid that they will upset the parents or they may feel that they do not know enough about the child and the disability. Teachers may decide that discussions related to the disability are better left to other professionals who specialize in that area.

One teacher remembered,

"I wanted to know if I could expect Marjorie to follow the same rules as the other children. I didn't know if I should expect her to help put the toys away at clean-up time. But I didn't want to ask her mother, because I was afraid she would think that Marjorie was misbehaving."

Another teacher commented,

"I noticed that Malcolm wasn't eating snacks, and he seemed unusually quiet. I wondered if his behavior might mean that something was wrong with his shunt, but I hesitated to mention it to his mother, because I didn't feel it was my place to discuss medical matters."

When directors and parents are reluctant to talk about difficult topics, they need to remember that the child's interests are best served by an honest and open sharing of information.

Ground Rules

Relationships do not happen overnight. They take time and attention to develop and flourish. Here are some guidelines to keep in mind whenever you talk to parents.

Create an Atmosphere of Trust and Understanding

Encourage a positive exchange of information. Ask parents what they want to know about their child's experience. Let them know that you are on their side and want to work with them to provide the best experience for their child. Consider scheduling a conference that includes you, as well as the teacher, shortly after the child enrolls to talk with the family about their expectations, goals, and concerns. This meeting can be a wonderful opportunity to get to know each other before any problem arises.

One parent commented,

"I was surprised when both the director and Johnny's teacher asked to meet with us. He had been at the center for just 2 weeks. They told us how he was adjusting and asked us what we hoped he would learn in the program. I really appreciated their interest. After that meeting, I knew they would take good care of Johnny, and I felt like I could talk to them whenever I had a question."

Communicate in a Variety of Ways

Notes, newsletters, informal conversations in the hall, telephone calls, and e-mail can help you establish frequent contact with all families. This regular communication strengthens your developing relationship with the family and helps parents and teachers gradually get to know each other better. It also helps parents feel that they are free to talk to you as well as the classroom teacher before their concerns escalate. One parent appreciated written information about her son.

"The weekly newsletter was so important to me. It was the only way I knew what activities were going to happen each day. It helped me know what to ask Jamal about when he came home."

Another parent said,

"I loved the notes that Margaret brought home from school. They were just a line or two, but they let me know how her day went. They reassured me that she was having fun, even though she couldn't tell me in so many words."

Take Time to Communicate with the Family

Think about communication from the parents' perspective. Imagine that you are the parent of a child with a disability who has difficulty communicating. Your child comes home from school, and he or she cannot tell you about her day. You worry about whether he or she ate her lunch, whether another child hit him or her, or if your child had a good time. As you think about communication from the parents' point of view, you can better understand why many parents desire as much information about their child as you can give them. When a child has difficulty communicating, the parent really has no idea what goes on each day unless the program tells him or her. Mom and Dad cannot talk about school with their child unless they know about some of the major events. It also will be easier to raise a difficult subject if you can communicate regularly with the family. Provide frequent short progress reports to let the parents know how things are going.

Focus on Strengths

Parents are used to hearing about what is wrong with their child. You need to build a relationship on the strengths of the family and the child, not on the weaknesses. Ask your teachers to let parents know about the small successes that they see on a daily basis. Parents appreciate hearing about the ways their child is similar to his or her peers without disabilities.

Jenny's mother reported,

"About 2 weeks after Jenny started school, her teacher called to tell me that she had used the slide for the first time that day. I can't tell you how much that short telephone call meant to me. The teacher really seemed to know Jenny and like her. After that, I started to relax and think that maybe Jenny did belong with regular kids after all."

Trust Yourself

As the director, you see the child daily, and through the teacher, you learn the child's likes, dislikes, routines, and unique characteristics. Do not underestimate how much you really do know about the child, and do not let the disability frighten you into thinking that you know less about this child than you do about the other children in your program. Parents do not expect you to be an expert in special education. In most situations, there will be several people who provide specialized services to the child that directly address the disability.

Parents want you to see to it that their child is safe, happy, and a valued member of the group. Your unique contribution is your knowledge of the child in the context of other children without disabilities. Your perspective allows you to see all the ways the child with a disability is similar to the children without disabilities. It is easier to establish open avenues of communication when you understand your role and what parents expect of you.

Respect the Individuality of Each Family

Each family comes with its own set of values and beliefs. If you can meet with the family shortly after their child enters the program, then you can talk with them about their expectations. It is important to appreciate and respect their values, goals, and concerns even when they are different from your own. Start with the assumption that parents want what is best for their child. They have the lifelong responsibility of caring for their child, and they have the right to make final decisions in all matters.

Keep Information Confidential

Talk with parents about your program philosophy and curriculum when they enroll their child in your program. Each family has its own values and beliefs, and each family needs to choose a program that is compatible with those values and beliefs. Let parents know that your program does not discriminate against children with disabilities. Provide them with information about **inclusion** and reassure them that each child gets the time and attention he or she needs. Show them how *all* children benefit by being educated together.

Parents also need to know how to respond to questions or comments that their child might ask at home. Provide information for them to use, so they will feel comfortable and so that children learn that their questions will get honest, consistent responses. Be receptive to parents' reports about what their child says about school when he or she is at home.

Sometimes parents of other children will ask you about the child with a disability. They may want to know how the child's presence is affecting the rest of the class. They might have specific questions about the disability, or they might want some information to help them talk with their own child about differences and disabilities. When this happens, give them the information they need without violating the privacy of the child with a disability and his or her family. Try to prepare for this possibility before it arises by asking the parents of a child with a disability how they would like you to handle questions. When other people ask questions about a child's disability, it is important to respect the child's privacy. By talking with parents about the issue before it arises, you can be prepared to respond in a manner consistent with the family's wishes.

If the family allows, then you can talk about the differences that other children and adults might notice. You will be able to explain why one child might not be able to run fast and will be able to respond to other questions that parents might ask. If necessary, you should ask parents how they would like you to handle other issues that might arise. For example, if a child uses any special equipment, such as braces or a walker, then his mother might come to school to talk with the other children and give them an opportunity to use the equipment. She could also provide written information for teachers to send home.

What Parents Want

It helps to understand the family's perspective as you begin to build positive relationships. Parents want you to recognize their efforts and respect the decisions they have made for their child.

Time

Most of all, parents want someone who will take the time to listen to them. Let them know that you will make time for their concerns. Consider scheduling a regular time that parents can reach you and the child's teacher by telephone. For example, you could let families know that they can reach you on Tuesdays between 1 p.m. and 2 p.m. Teachers might offer to return telephone calls one evening a week (e.g., Wednesdays between 8:30 p.m. and 9 p.m.). You also could set aside one afternoon a week for parents to talk with you briefly. It may be easier for you to communicate via e-mail or telephone.

Information

Parents need clear, accurate, and complete information on the center, the classroom, and their child's activities, but they do not expect you to know everything about their child. When you do not know, admit it. Make sure your teachers are comfortable as well. Parents do expect you to talk with them honestly and openly. They want straight answers, not jargon or evasion. One mother explained,

"I asked Caleb's teacher for some ideas for toilet training him. She said that she didn't really know anything specific for children with Down syndrome, but she would see what she could find out. A few days later she told me that she had spoken with her director and gave me the telephone number of a behavior specialist and a brochure on toilet training. It made me realize that the program really does care about Caleb, and they are on my side."

Care and Compassion

Parents may have had experiences in which their child was not accepted, and they may have received a lot of bad news from professionals. You can help by recognizing their concerns. Your willingness to talk openly communicates that you care about their feelings and that you want what is best for their child.

What Teachers Need

Teachers want and need many of the same things as parents. They need to build a relationship with the child and his or her family. As the director, you will lead this process. Let parents know how they can help you. Following are some issues that you might talk about.

Information

Teachers need to know information about the child and family that might affect the child in the classroom. If parents understand why you need this information, then they will be more willing to discuss things with you.

Trust

When the teacher asks about the child's disability, you want the family to trust that he or she will not misuse the information or treat the child inappropriately. Let the family know that the teacher will use the information for the good of the child.

Feedback

Everyone needs to be appreciated. You can establish mechanisms to acknowledge the skills and professionalism of your teachers. Let parents know how they can help. Communication works both ways. You let parents know what happens in school, and you and your teachers need to know what happens at home. How does the child feel about coming to school? How do the parents feel about what is happening in the classroom?

Planning a Parent Conference

When it is time for a formal conference with a child's parents, it can be helpful to think through the process with the teacher in advance. Find out what parents want to discuss and what questions they have. Then work with the teacher to gather the necessary information, including reports on the child, information from other professionals, or community resources with names and telephone numbers. You might also want to review the meeting in advance with the teacher.

• Who will be at the conference?

• What do you want to tell the parents?

- What will you say first?

- How do you think they will react?

- How would you feel if you were the parent in this situation?

- What do you want the outcome of the conference to be?

Finally, schedule a convenient time and find a quiet, private space to meet. Let parents know the purpose of the meeting in advance, and, in families with two parents, encourage both parents to attend. It is also helpful to clarify how long the conference will last.

Guidelines for the Conference

- Start the conference on a positive note. Tell a short anecdote about something good the child has done in the classroom.

- Avoid jargon. State the reason for wanting to talk with the parents in plain language.

- Give examples of what you see in the classroom. Be specific, and do not make assumptions or jump to conclusions.

- Invite the parents to tell you how they see their child.

- Work with the parents to develop a plan of action to address the problem. Try to have referral numbers and books or other resources available.

- Remember that the parents may be just as nervous as you.

- Give information, not advice.

- Take notes and write down the main points that were discussed so you can refer to them later.

- Summarize at the end of the meeting and decide with the parents on the next steps.

Even if you follow these guidelines, there will still be times when the conference does not go well, and parents become upset or angry. But talking with parents on a regular basis will make it easier to bring up difficult subjects. Remember that parents want to know that you care about their child. They want you to be sensitive as well as honest. Regular communication will help you do a better job in the program and it will help the parents do a better job at home. When directors, teachers, and parents work together, the child has a better chance for a positive school experience.

9

Supporting Staff to Talk About Disabilities with Children and Parents

> **Key Concepts:** person-first language

Children and adults notice and comment when they see a person who looks or acts different. When children with disabilities are included in your program, the other children and parents will have questions about those differences. Differences are what make each person unique. These differences are not necessarily good or bad; these differences are simply characteristics that make us individuals. By acknowledging and accepting variations in age, language, race, size, religion, family composition, and cultural background, you can help everyone see both similarities and variations.

One kind of difference is a disability. If teachers respond to questions about disabilities with clear and accurate information, teachers let children and parents know that it is all right to talk openly about differences. Their words provide a positive model that others can use to talk sensitively and respectfully about differences and disabilities. The answers help people learn about and understand those differences. Talking about differences, including disabilities, helps all of the children and their families. Talking about differences also gives children and their families important information and lets them know that your program values and accepts each individual.

The adults and children in your program may already embody diversity. Differences should not overshadow the many things that the children with and without disabilities and their families have in common.

Children with disabilities are children first and are more alike than different from their peers. They share many of the same likes and dislikes as other children, and they need to have friends who care about them and who accept them as valuable members of the community.

Person-First Language

When you and your staff talk about anyone who has a disability, it is important to put the person before the special need. A label or diagnosis describes the disability. It does not tell you what he or she is like, what he or she thinks, or what he or she can do. When you put the person first you speak of "the child who has a disability." This puts the emphasis on the person rather than on the disability. Using a descriptive term may give more information than a diagnosis. Say, "Jenny has trouble walking," rather than "Jenny has cerebral palsy." This is called **person-first language.**

Use the correct name for the disability. For example, *Down syndrome* is the accepted term, rather than *mongoloid*. Of course, do not use pejorative words, such as *retard*. Try to avoid generalizations that tend to glorify the disability, such as "Children with mental retardation are always so happy," or "People with a visual impairment compensate for their loss by developing a better sense of hearing." There is as much variation among people within a disability category as there is within the general population. Describing the disability does not describe the person.

The same rule applies when you talk about any equipment or devices that a person with a disability uses. Refer to a person as using a wheelchair instead of saying, "He or she is wheelchair bound." Talk about a child who wears a hearing aid rather than referring to that child as an "aided child."

What Children Notice

Infants and toddlers notice obvious differences in faces. For example, some babies will cry if a stranger approaches. They may be frightened by a man with a beard who looks different from their clean-shaven father. Babies like to watch other children, but they do not seem disturbed by general physical differences in less familiar people.

Children who are 2 and 3 years old notice physical differences but do not always have the verbal ability to ask questions or comment on what they see. Staff and family members may be able to tell by their facial expressions or behavior when children are trying to make sense out of the differences they see and hear. For example, a child may have a concerned look on his or her face when he or she sees a child return after having chickenpox. The child notices the marks and is trying to make sense out of what he or she sees. A child may be unwilling to hold hands or sit near another child whose behavior or appearance is unusual.

Older children both observe and comment on differences. Some of the first differences they notice are those differences that are visible. These may be physical abilities, such as the way a person walks or uses his or her hands, or physical characteristics, such as size, facial appearance, or the absence of limbs. As children become more sophisticated, they notice differences in behavior and language, such as frequent temper tantrums, crying, unusual speech or lack of speech.

Children do not automatically think that differences are bad, but they do ask questions and make comments as they try to understand what they see. They look to the adults around them for signs of how to react. Teachers and family members can help the children talk about differences and similarities and help them understand what these differences and similarities mean.

How Children Think

When you talk to children about disabilities, keep in mind that they do not think like adults. Their questions about disabilities reflect their intellectual level of development. They have had fewer experiences in the world that they can use to understand what they see, and they rely on adults to provide them with honest, accurate information.

Some children may think that a disability happens because the person did something wrong. For example, a young child might think that a person cannot hear because he or she is being punished. A teacher or parent can explain that deafness is not anyone's fault. It happens when a person's ears do not work. When they see a person with a disability, they may think, "Will it happen to me? Can I catch it? How did that happen?" Saying things, such as "Deafness isn't like a cold. You can't catch it," can help a child understand what he or she is experiencing. Young children have a concrete understanding of cause and effect. They relate everything to themselves.

Young children have a limited understanding of past and future time and do not understand what "forever" means. To many young children, things that happened in the past were "yesterday." Things that will happen in the future are "tomorrow." Everything else is "today" or "later." Young children often do not understand that a disability is permanent.

When told that a child is blind and cannot see, a child may say, "Well, she'll get to see it tomorrow." Rather than arguing about "forever," it is more important that the child understand about "right now." You might say, "Every day you will see Tameka, but she won't be able to see you."

Even after answering the questions, adults may have to answer the same question tomorrow or next week. Children are trying to understand new ideas that puzzle them, and their understanding takes time. Children's thinking changes as they get older. At each new stage of development, they need to hear an honest answer that matches their level of understanding.

Communicating Positive Values About People with Disabilities

The children in your program will follow the example of the adults in their lives. Be clear about the acceptance of diversity modeled and taught in your classrooms.

- Is diversity welcomed?

- Are differences embraced and celebrated?

- Are each child's unique abilities recognized?

- Are examples of diversity included throughout the classroom in pictures, toys, and books?

In some classrooms, a different child is featured each week. A picture is put up on the bulletin board and the child and family share information about themselves during that week. This activity honors and shows respect for every family in the program.

Another way to introduce children to people with disabilities is to invite classroom visitors who can talk to the children. For example, you might invite an adult who is visually impaired to talk with the class and explain how he or she uses a guide dog and walking stick to get around. It is important with any awareness activities that the children have a chance to ask questions both at the time of the activity and for several weeks afterward.

Children watch how adults react when someone is hurt or teased. Help children verbalize their feelings and think about how others feel. To some children, tones of voice are more important than the specific words adults use. Let children know that even though each of them is different, they are all important and valued members of the class. Teach empathy and respect. Children can learn to listen to each other and understand how others feel. As one young girl in the videotape *Regular Lives* explained, "Just because you can't walk or talk doesn't mean that you don't have feelings" (State of the Art, Inc., 1994).

It helps children to recognize what they have in common with each other and with the child who has a disability. Encourage the teachers to talk about everyone who has a baby brother or who likes ice cream. Find common ground to help children see what characteristics they share and that a disability is just one part of a person. This helps children recognize that although they are each different, they are all capable and important. Talk about the things each child does well; then, talk about things that are hard to learn.

Guidelines for Answering Children's Questions About Differences

Children ask questions about things they can see and experience directly. As an administrator or a parent, children probably have asked you difficult questions. Children are quite candid and may make comments that surprise you. They also can ask embarrassing questions when you least expect it. Be prepared! Children have inquiring minds, and they ask questions to learn about their world. They think about the answers you give them and may come back to you to ask more questions and get more information at a later time. Young children accept simple, factual information. Not responding to a child's questions may lead a child to believe that what he or she asked about should not be discussed or that there is something wrong about the question. For example, if a child in the classroom asks, "What's the matter with her?" teachers could simply state, "There's nothing the matter. Amy is not able to walk, so she uses a special chair to get around." Teachers can help all of the children understand about a classmate who is blind by explaining that "Miguel's eyes don't work well, so he uses his ears and hands to know where things are." Teachers can use these opportunities as a chance to communicate information and the positive values discussed in this chapter.

Children absorb information in small doses. They may want a simple explanation without extensive details. Responses should be direct and simple explanations with examples that the children can understand. For instance, a child may ask, "How come he can't talk?" A teacher might answer, "Johnny doesn't talk with words, but he can talk with his hands. Here, let me show you." Another question may be, "How come she's so short?" Your answer might be, "Laurie's body grows more slowly. No one in our class is exactly the same size. We all grow differently."

Using descriptive words helps a child understand what he or she is experiencing. Try to think of an explanation that is something the child might have experienced. For example, you may say to the child, "Remember when you wore your earmuffs in the winter, and it was hard to hear what I was saying? That is what Jennifer hears most of the time," or "Think about what you see at night. It's dark, and you can only see shapes and a little light. That's what seeing is like for Michael."

Look at the expression on a child's face. Watch his or her body language, and listen to the tone of his or her voice. Does he or she have a question but not know how to ask it? Remember that children notice differences even if they do not always talk about them. Children sometimes have a hard time finding the words to express what they are thinking. You may have to ask the questions when you see a child react but does not ask a question or comment. If a child looks fearful and shies away from a person, you might comment, "That man's hand looks scary to you, doesn't it?"

At other times, adults might see a child staring. This is an opportunity to use the "some children" technique. For example, a teacher can say, "Some children wonder if wearing a brace hurts," or "Some children wonder how you get into a car in a wheelchair. Do you wonder about that?" Then you can provide the answer, such as the following: "Sometimes a person has to be picked up and moved into the car, and sometimes a person can stand and sit down in the car. Other people have special cars, and the wheelchair rolls into the car."

Differences can be frightening or upsetting when they are not understood. Acknowledging and labeling children's reactions can help their understanding. For example, "I noticed that you didn't want to sit next to Brian. It scares me when he screams. Does it scare you, too? He needs our help to learn to use words. Let's tell him that his screaming frightens us." In another situation, you might say, "I know it makes you sad when Felicia won't play with you, but right now Felicia can't run. She needs to rest. Let's invite her to play after naptime."

Children learn by watching others and noting their reactions. They hear how words are spoken and see how attitudes are demonstrated through facial expression and body language. Caring, empathetic teachers can demonstrate that these qualities are valued in others. It is a good way to teach children to care about and help each other. For example, you could tell the children in your program the following: "We are going to walk down the hallway in pairs quietly. It helps the children in the other classes to work if we are quiet. Be good friends and remind each other how to walk quietly."

If staff and family members understand how children think, the answers they give to their questions provide teaching opportunities for learning about others with sensitivity and caring.

Talking with Parents

Talk with parents about your program philosophy and curriculum when they enroll their child in your program. Each family has its own values and beliefs and needs to choose a program that is compatible with those values and beliefs. Let parents know that your program does not discriminate against children with disabilities. Provide parents with information about inclusion and reassure them that each child gets the time and attention he or she needs. Show them how *all* children benefit by being educated together.

Parents also need to know how to respond to questions or comments that their child might ask at home. Share the information in this chapter with parents. Work with parents so that children learn that their questions will get honest, consistent responses. Be receptive to parents' reports about what their child says about school when he or she is at home. Parents of children with disabilities have been answering questions about their children since the birth of their children. Ask them for suggestions about how to answer questions and what information they would like others to know about their child. Some children with disabilities are also used to being asked questions and prefer to give their own answers.

Privacy and Confidentiality

All families have the right to privacy and confidentiality about personal information. It is very important to maintain that confidentiality. Although there may be questions about the child with a disability from parents or other staff, no information about the child is disclosed unless specific permission has been given by the family. Some suggestions to assist in developing policies and procedures include the following:

1. Provide clear and comprehensible information about the acceptance of diversity in your program.

2. Provide support and information to your staff about answering questions about disabilities in developmentally appropriate ways.

3. Be available to answer parents' questions about the presence of children with disabilities in your program.

4. Enforce a clear policy about maintaining confidentiality of information about all families.

All children deserve courtesy and respect and should be valued for who they are. Children with disabilities are more alike than different from other children. Teachers can help children value each other by communicating positively about differences and answering children's questions appropriately.

10

Collaborating with Special Education Providers

> **Key Concepts:** Child Find; occupational therapy services; physical therapy services; speech-language services

Section I described the ADA and related laws that were historical precedents and ensured people with disabilities that they would receive civil rights and an education. Many children are eligible for and receive special education services through their public school system. You can gain access to resources for children in your program by understanding the federal, state, and local special education laws and how they work in your community. It is important to try to form a collaborative relationship with any other program that provides services for the child with disabilities. This chapter explains the special education process and what role you might provide in helping coordinate services for the child and family.

Child Find

Child Find is one of the services provided by all local public school systems that identifies young children with disabilities and helps them obtain special education services if they qualify. "States must ensure that all children with disabilities living in the State, including children in private schools, regardless of the severity of their disability, and who need special education and related services, are identified, located, and evaluated" (IDEA 2004, Sec. 300.111, 2006 Regulations).

Parents who have a child between 3 and 5 years old (younger children may be eligible, depending on state and local regulations) can contact Child Find in the special education division of their local public school system if they have concerns about their child's development. Look in the local telephone directory for the local public school system for the child. Call the general information number or the special education services number to get the Child Find listing. They will provide screening and assessment at no cost for children who may have a disability and be in need of special education services. When you suspect that a child has special learning needs, refer the parents to Child Find for an assessment. Anyone can make a referral to Child Find, but parents or guardians must give permission for any testing and evaluation. If parents decide to seek a screening and evaluation through Child Find services, then they need to call and make an appointment. Parents also have the option of seeking a private evaluation. As the administrator, you can help smooth the way by having information available to give to parents. Your local Child Find office can provide you with brochures.

Screening and Evaluation

Special education laws provide specific due process procedures and protections to parents. Parents must give written permission before their child can be assessed, and testing must be conducted in the child's native language. Parents may also request that any conferences be held in their native language. Parents have the right to know what types of assessment will be done, the length of the assessments, and how long it will take to get the results. A screening is often done first to determine if a full evaluation is needed. A full evaluation is conducted by a multidisciplinary team that includes a teacher and at least one other specialist who is knowledgeable about the suspected area of disability. Any test given must be free of racial or cultural bias. This multidisciplinary team may also include a psychologist; a special educator; and other service providers, such as occupational, physical, and SLPs. Parents may be asked to sign a release so that the school system may obtain information from other sources, such as hospitals or doctors. As the program administrator, you also have valuable information that can help in screening and evaluating the child. You and the classroom teacher may be asked to provide a written report describing the child and detailing your concerns. Parents have the right to seek an independent evaluation if they disagree with the results of the testing.

The school system should also provide parents with information about the process that follows the evaluation. After the testing is complete, an eligibility meeting will be held to determine if their child will be found eligible for special education services. If their child is eligible, then the parents and the multidisciplinary team write a plan to guide the provision of education and related services (i.e., IEP, IFSP). Based on the IEP or IFSP, parents and personnel from the school system decide what classroom or placement would best provide the services needed. The services must begin according to the time line determined by federal law and state guidelines, which is usually within 45 days of the determination of eligibility. A child 3 or older who is eligible for special education services must be provided those services free of charge in a public program. In some states, services for children under age 3 may be provided on a sliding scale fee for service.

Special Education Services

Children who are found eligible for special education services can receive a variety of services in a range of settings. The services a child receives is determined by the IFSP (for infants through age 2, depending on local regulations) or the IEP (for children over age 3). A meeting is held to write a plan specifying learning goals and special education services. Parents are allowed to invite anyone they wish to the meeting and, if feasible, you or the classroom teacher should consider participating in this meeting. The people at the meeting review all of the available information about the child and develop appropriate learning goals or outcomes. The IEP and IFSP specify the learning goals, how progress toward the goals will be measured, and when services will begin and end.

The Individualized Family Service Plan Meeting

An IFSP meeting includes the parents or guardian, anyone invited by the parents, the service coordinator, and service providers. The IFSP must include the following components:

- A statement of the infant's or toddler's present levels of development (physical, cognitive, speech-language, psychosocial, motor, and self-help)
- A statement of the family's resources, priorities, and concerns related to the child's development
- A statement of major outcomes expected to be achieved for the child and the family through early intervention
- The criteria, procedures, and time lines for determining progress

- The specific early intervention services necessary to meet the unique needs of the child and family, including the frequency, intensity, and method of delivering services in natural environments

- The projected dates for initiating services and expected duration of those services

- The name of the service coordinator

- Procedures for transition from early intervention into the preschool program

Every locality has its own format for an IFSP, but the information listed previously should be included, and the family should be very involved in deciding what kind of a program they would like for their child. Appendix A at the end of this chapter contains an example of an IFSP.

The Individualized Education Program Meeting

When a child is found eligible for services, an IEP meeting is held within 30 calendar days to share information about the child and develop a plan that will guide and document the provision of all special education services. An IEP meeting should include the parents or guardian; the child's teacher(s); an administrative representative of the school other than the child's teacher; other individuals, at the discretion of the school or the parents (e.g., the evaluators); and the child, when appropriate. An IEP must include the following components:

- A statement of the child's current educational performance levels

- Annual goals and short-term objectives

- A description of the specific special education and related services to be provided

- A statement of the extent to which the child will be able to participate in regular education programs

- The date on which services will begin and their anticipated duration

- Appropriate objective evaluation criteria and evaluation procedures and schedules for determining, at least annually, whether the short-term objectives are being achieved

- A statement of need for technology devices or services, if appropriate

At this meeting, alternatives for placement, including community options, may be considered and discussed to determine which are the most appropriate. A parent must give written consent before a child is placed in a special education program. Appendix B at the end of this chapter contains an example of an IEP.

Both the IEP and IFSP must outline the kinds of services that the child is to receive based on that child's needs. Descriptions of the most frequently encountered services follow.

Special Education

Special education is specially designed instruction, provided at no cost to parents, that meets a child's unique needs. These services are usually provided by someone who has been trained in special education. Using the IEP/IFSP, the special educator develops specific activities to enhance the child's learning and minimize the effect of any disabling condition, collects data to monitor the child's progress, and makes suggestions for adapting the regular curriculum to meet the child's learning needs. Special education services can be provided in a classroom, home, hospital, or other setting. Special education also includes related services.

Related Services

Related services are transportation and other developmental, corrective, and support services required to assist a child with a disability. Whether a child receives them depends on what the child needs. The special education laws include a list of services to help a child benefit from special education, such as audiology; psychological services; medical services for diagnostic or evaluation purposes only; school health services; recreation, including therapeutic recreation; counseling services; early identification and assessment of disabilities; social work; parent counseling; and training. Three of the most common services are described next.

Speech-Language Services

Speech-language services are provided by an SLP who specializes in communication disorders, such as voice quality, pronunciation (articulation), oral motor skills, vocabulary (language), and hearing. Oral motor skills refer to the way the muscles of the mouth and face work. Speech-language therapy helps a child develop and use language. An SLP can also help develop augmentative and alternative communication (AAC) for children who need to communicate using pictures, signs, or computers instead of speech. Under the ADA, these communication systems may serve as auxiliary aids and services.

Physical Therapy Services

Physical therapy services help a child develop and use motor skills related to coordination, balance, muscle strength, endurance, range of motion, and mobility. The physical therapist develops specific exercises to help a child learn to move the large muscles of his or her body for activities such as crawling, walking, running, jumping, and climbing. The therapist may also make specific suggestions for special equipment, such as braces, wheelchairs, or walkers, to help a child learn to move as independently as possible.

Occupational Therapy Services

Occupational therapy services help children in fine motor, oral motor, perceptual/motor, sensory processing, and daily living activities. The occupational therapist may use activities to help the child organize incoming information from all of the senses (visual, tactile, auditory, balance). Sensory information combined appropriately with movement results in better quality skills for many play, learning, and self-help activities. The occupational therapist helps children learn to use crayons, markers, paintbrushes, or similar items for writing and drawing; use the playground equipment; complete puzzles; and participate in art activities. Daily living activities, such as learning to eat, dress, and use the bathroom independently, might also be part of a child's occupational therapy program.

Collaboration

Your local school system can be an important source of information and support as you include children with disabilities in your program. When a child in your program is found eligible for special education services, you may ask to participate in the IEP or IFSP meetings and obtain copies of the documents with the parents' permission. The information in the IFSP or IEP can help you adapt activities to meet the child's needs. If a child attends both a special education program and an early childhood program, then it is important that both programs communicate with each other regularly so that educational expectations can be coordinated. In addition to e-mail and telephone calls, a low-tech strategy is to start a communication notebook that the child carries in a book bag. Parents, teachers, and therapists can make entries in the notebook about daily activities, and they can ask and answer questions. This way everyone can stay informed about the child's progress.

Integrated Services

One of the most effective ways to provide services to children with disabilities is to make them part of the regular classroom routine. As much as possible, therapeutic activities should have a clear purpose for the child during his or her daily routine. For example, dressing skills should be practiced when coats are put on and taken off before and after going outside. This promotes learning in a natural context. This type of service delivery requires time to coordinate the planning, implement the program, and monitor progress. It may fall to you as the program administrator to initiate this effort.

Consultative Services

Many school systems provide special education services in community programs. Special education personnel may be available to meet with the child's teacher to plan and coordinate his or her program. This consultation may be in addition to, or in lieu of, providing direct services to the child. For example, an SLP from the public schools may be available to meet with a child's classroom teacher to discuss goals and teaching strategies. Some school systems will also provide direct special education services to the child while he or she is in a community-based program.

Obtaining Special Education Services

There are many steps in applying for and obtaining special education services. The family and child need your support as they make their way through this process. It is frustrating for everyone when the school system process seems to move slowly, so it helps if parents and teachers understand how the school system works and how to be good advocates by persisting in seeking the services their children need.

Public school systems are moving toward providing more opportunities for children to receive services in natural environments and integrated placements. Parents are asking school systems to support a continuum of inclusive opportunities for their children with disabilities by providing special education services in regular early childhood programs. Successful inclusive services for all children depend on cooperation, coordination, and collaboration between public schools and private community programs.

10

Chapter Appendix A

Individualized
Family
Service Plan

Child's name: David Smith
Date of birth: February 13, 2007

Service coordinator: Sue Simon, M.S.W.
Telephone number: 608-123-5555
Referral date: November 5, 2007
Initial IFSP date: December 12, 2007

IFSP review date(s):

1) _____ 2) _____ 3) _____ 4) _____ 5) _____ 6) _____
a) _____ a) _____ a) _____ a) _____ a) _____ a) _____
b) _____ b) _____ b) _____ b) _____ b) _____ b) _____
c) _____ c) _____ c) _____ c) _____ c) _____ c) _____

All About *David Smith*

Child lives with: *Jane and John Smith*   Other parent/guardian name (if applicable):

Relationship: *Parents*
Address: *111 Main Street*   Address:
Somewhere, WI 12345
Home telephone: *608-123-4567*   Home telephone:
Alternate telephone: Alternate telephone:
E-mail: E-mail:

Other parent/guardian (if different from above):
Address: Telephone:
Primary language of parents: *English*   Primary language of child: *English*
Spends day with:

[X] Mom   [ ] Child care provider: _____

[ ] Dad   [ ] Other (Specify): _____

Siblings:

Other important people or information:

Primary medical care provider/medical home: *Dr. K, Pediatric Physicians, 1111 North St, Somewhere, WI 12345*

Services and programs my child/family currently uses:

[ ] Badger Care   [ ] Health department

[ ] Support groups   [ ] Healthy Start

[ ] Department of Human Services   [ ] Library

[ ] Family Resource Center   [ ] Support groups

[ ] Family Support   [ ] Medical Assistance

[ ] Head Start   [ ] Other: _____

We want more information about the following programs: _____
_____

Tell Us About Your Family

What is going well for your child and family right now?

David continues to acquire new skills daily in the area of communication. He has made some progress with "scootching" and is more solid when bearing weight.

What is your family concerned or interested in learning more about?

Gross motor development

People or supports that are helpful to your family:

David attends Kindermusic on Thursday mornings at 9:15 a.m. David's parents share two nannies with a friend and her child.

What are some activities you enjoy doing with your child and family?

David really likes being with people and loves music and dancing. He is very social.

What would you like to see happen for your child and family in the next 6 months?

Walking independently

Activities or times of day that are difficult or stressful for your child and family:

Best times for visits are between 11 a.m. and 2 p.m. He naps between 45 and 90 minutes twice a day (9 a.m. to 10:30 a.m. and 2 p.m. to 3 p.m.).

Summary of All Developmental Areas

(For use with the Early Intervention Team Report and IFSP)

Name: *David Smith*   Date of report: *11/28/07*

Date of birth: *2/13/07*

Age at evaluation: *9 months*   Adjusted age: *N/A*

List tools, strategies, and locations used to determine status in each area.

PHYSICAL DEVELOPMENT

HEALTH
(includes medical and dental)

Jane's pregnancy with David was quite difficult. She suffered from both anemia and gestational diabetes, which was controlled with diet. Due to concerns about David's growth in utero, Jane was on bed rest for the final 5 weeks of her pregnancy until David's birth at 37 weeks. At birth, David weighed 4 pounds, 8 ounces, and was diagnosed as having intrauterine growth retardation and being small for gestational age. David remained in the neonatal intensive care unit (NICU) for 3 days due to problems maintaining his temperature. David had difficulties gaining weight, so for the first 2 months he was fed pumped breast milk supplemented with formula. David's 9-month exam revealed he is severely anemic. He's currently on iron supplements and is starting to eat meat. He will have follow-up testing for the anemia soon. He also takes medication for acid reflux. His immunizations are up to date.

VISION/HEARING
(screening, glasses, hearing aids, history of ear infections)

David passed his newborn hearing screening. There are no concerns about his hearing or vision at this time.

Fine motor skills: *A child's ability to use the small muscles in his or her hands, including hand–eye coordination*

There are no parental concerns regarding this area of David's development. His mother shared that David enjoys exploring toys with his eyes and hands, and he also uses his hands well to self-feed a variety of foods. David also likes to hold a spoon during feedings. During the evaluation visit, David sat on the floor and played with a variety of age-appropriate toys. He demonstrated a well-developing "radial digital" grasp (using the side of his thumbs against his fingertips) to pick up small toys. He was able to reach for toys with an extended elbow with good accuracy. He is just starting to bang toys together, which is considered an 8.5- to 12-month skill. David isn't yet dropping objects purposefully during container play, which is considered an 8- to 10-month skill.

Findings

Based on parent report and direct observations, David is showing fine motor skills that are solid through the 8.5-month level, with skills in the 9- to 11-month range emerging. At this time, his fine motor skills are within the normal range for his age.

Next steps for fine motor skills

1. Dropping small toys/blocks into pots or pans to hear the noise

2. Banging toys on different objects

3. Poking at objects with his index fingers

4. Using a "neat pincer grasp" of his thumb pads against his fingertips

Sensorimotor

David's parents have observed that David is more sensitive to sudden and/or loud sounds than many children in his age group. During the evaluation, David did startle easily in response to louder voices or laughter, but he recovered quickly when reassured by his mother. His parents have him participating in some group activities that he enjoys (e.g., swim lessons, Kindermusic, Book Baby), which seems to be helping him become more comfortable with higher levels of sensory stimulation. He enjoys visually exploring his environment, which was observed during the evaluation. He appears to be comfortable with different materials and foods on his hands. David accepts a variety of food flavors and participates in self-feeding. He enjoys bath time. David is a very calm child who loves to be held and rocked. David does not show a strong drive to physically explore his environment and to experience novel movement sensations. He appears most comfortable sitting and playing. When he was briefly handled and moved through different positions during the evaluation, he showed some distress and cried but recovered with comfort from his mother.

Findings

David shows typically developing sensorimotor skills in several areas; however, he does show some differences in his responses to auditory input and to movement experiences. His reluctance to initiate gross motor movements appears to be contributing to a moderate delay in this area of development.

Gross motor

Mr. and Mrs. Smith shared that they are concerned with David's gross motor development because he's not crawling or pulling to stand. David does not transition from one position to another or only does so with difficulty. His parents are concerned that David's anemia affects his energy levels and, thus, his interest in developing further motor skills. During the evaluation visit, David was seated on a blanket. He showed a stable sitting posture with good spine extension. He did not initiate any movements out of sitting, nor did he perform any rotational movements of his trunk to reach for toys. When he was placed in a prone position, he shifted his weight to one side to reach for a toy in front of him. David does now move a short distance with his tummy down on the floor, but is not actively crawling. At this time, David does not enjoy standing on his feet while being supported or standing at stable furniture.

Findings

Based on parent report and direct observations, at 9 months of age David is showing most gross motor skills through the 7-month level, with some skills at the 8-month range emerging. Some important skills in the 4- to 6-month range, such as rolling, are not well established. At this time, David's gross motor skills are delayed approximately 25% for his age.

COMMUNICATION
(understanding, expression, intelligibility, pragmatics)

Language comprehension: A child's ability to understand what is said to him or her

There are no parental concerns in this area of David's development. David enjoys peekaboo, raises his hands when he wants to picked up and in response to "touchdown," and waves a little bit in response to "bye-bye." During the evaluation, David looked at the person saying his name and maintained his attention to the speaker. He also attended to pictures and music. David responded to sounds when the source was not visible.

Findings

Based on the Rossetti Infant-Toddler Language Scale, David demonstrated language comprehension skills solid at the 6- to 9-month level with skills emerging into the 9- to 12-month level. This indicates age-appropriate language comprehension skills.

Language expression

There are no parental concerns in this area of David's development. His parents shared that he's recently become a much more vocal child, babbling and demonstrating turn taking in conversation. During the evaluation, David vocalized his feelings through intonation and took turns vocalizing. He initiated "talking" with the evaluators and would whine with a manipulative purpose. David will vocalize to gain attention and with communicative intent.

Findings

Based on the Rossetti Infant-Toddler Language Scale, David demonstrated language expression skills solid at the 6- to 9-month level with skills emerging into the 9- to 12-month level. This indicates age-appropriate language expression skills.

Oral-motor/articulation: A child's ability to use muscles in his or her mouth to eat and talk

David receives his nutrition from breastfeeding, baby food prepared by Mom, and some finger foods. David accepts a wide variety of foods and eats them without coughing or choking. David is exploring toys using his mouth and does not drool. Sounds heard or reported during the evaluation include a variety of vowel sounds; the letters m, b, d, h, and g; and raspberries. David has been heard playing with his vocal volume.

Findings

Based on parent report and observation, David demonstrated age-appropriate oral-motor skills.

COGNITION
(thinking skills, play skills, sensory skills)

David smiled during play activities today and played with a variety of age-appropriate toys. He interacted with objects and the people in his environment. David imitated play activities and participated in turn-taking games. He reached for himself in a mirror and tried to secure an object out of reach. When an object rolled behind him, David found it without difficulty. David's mother shared that David enjoys peekaboo.

Findings

Based on the Rossetti Infant-Toddler Language Scale, David demonstrated play skills solid at the 6- to 9-month level, with skills emerging into the 9- to 12-month level. This indicates age-appropriate play skills.

SOCIOEMOTIONAL
(engagement, response to caregivers, coping, sensory)

David's parents shared that David is usually happy and playful and loves to be held and cuddled. David does well with his nanny and also handles transitions between caregivers without distress. David's parents shared that David takes quite a bit of time to warm up to new people, and he is sensitive to loud voices and sudden sounds. It should be noted that he is at the age when children very often show "stranger anxiety." During the evaluation, David did startle easily in response to the evaluators' voices, but he recovered when reassured by his mother. He did interact cautiously in some play activities with the unfamiliar adults.

Findings

David shows typically developing socioemotional skills in most areas. He is quite shy with new people, which is not unusual for his age. He is sensitive to unfamiliar and/or sudden noises. His parents are providing excellent opportunities for David to interact socially with children and adults.

SELF-HELP
(feeding, dressing, toileting, adaptive skills)

Feeding: David is breastfed. He also self-feeds a wide variety of finger foods and likes to hold the spoon during meals.

Sleeping: David is able to fall asleep on his own with a short familiar bedtime routine. He awakens about every 2 hours at night. Currently, he does require some assistance from his parents to resettle to sleep when he awakens in the night. A pacifier is soothing to him. Currently, his nap times are rather irregular, with two to three naps each day.

Daily cares: *David tolerates daily cares well, such as bathing, diapering, and dressing.*

Findings

Based on parent report and direct observations, at 9 months of age, David is showing age-appropriate self-help skills.

Early Intervention Team Report

Early Intervention Eligibility Determination

Child's name: *David Smith*

This child meets the eligibility criteria for early intervention services (Check 1 or 2):

[X] 1 A) A developmental delay of 25% or greater or -1.3 standard deviation in the following area(s): *gross motor development*

   B) Atypical development based on _____
   _____
   _____

[ ] 2 A diagnosed physical or mental condition exists that has a high probability of resulting in a developmental delay. Specify condition(s) and source of diagnosis: _____
   _____
   _____

This child does not meet eligibility criteria for early intervention services:

* Offer to rescreen the child within 6 months.

   Notes: _____
   _____
   _____

* The following community resources might benefit the family: _____
   _____
   _____

* The following information was given to the family: _____
   _____
   _____

Participants in early intervention team meeting:

Mary Smith
_____
Parent/guardian signature

_____
Parent/guardian signature

Dan Nelson
_____
Service coordinator signature

Child and Family Outcome

We want: (What will happen or change?)

David to develop gross motor skills

So that: (Why is this important?)

He can explore his environment independently

What is already happening? (What is the child doing now? What has been tried? What is working?)

He does not like tummy time but is making some progress with "scootching."
He continues to acquire communication skills daily.

We will know we are successful when: (What can we observe or measure?)

David does some crawling, pulls to stand, cruises along furniture, moves
between different positions, and walks independently.

What will happen within the child and family's everyday routines and activities and places?	Notes
1. Guide David through movements. Starting on a bed may be easier at first. Movements should be in both directions.	
2. Increase tummy time. You can start with David lying on your chest and gradually recline further back. Provide him with little bits of tummy time throughout the day.	
3. You can also place David over your ankle as another means to provide him with tummy time.	
4. Assigned physical therapist to provide ongoing strategies.	

Date reviewed:

Describe progress toward outcome (circle one):

Accomplished   Continue   No longer important

Early Intervention Services to Help

David's Development

	Birth to 3 services				
Service	Start/end dates	Location	Frequency	Intensity	Funding sources
Service coordination	12/12/07	Home/child care	As needed	As needed	Birth to 3: county
Physical therapy	1/02/08	Home/child care	Once a week	1 hour	NA

If services will not be provided in a natural environment, please include a statement of why and the steps to be taken to get back to a natural environment. _____

Needed Medical and Other Services

(These are resources, supports, or services that assist the family but are not funded by Birth to 3.)

Supports needed	Who will help	Steps taken	Funding source
None at this time			

☐ IFSP team discussion found that no medical or other services were identified at this time.
Comment: _____

Team Signature Page

- I/we have received a copy of and understand the parent and child rights.
- This plan reflects the outcomes that are important to my child and family.
- I/we give consent for the services described in this IFSP for my child and family.
- I understand that this plan will be shared with all team members listed below so we can work in partnership on behalf of my family.

Mary Smith   12/12/07

Parent/guardian signature   Date

Parent/guardian signature   Date

Parent/guardian signature   Date reviewed

We have worked together with the family to create this IFSP and agree that this plan will guide our work.

Other IFSP team members names and signatures	Date	Other IFSP team members names and signatures	Date
Service coordinator:		Team member:	
Team member: _Dan Nelson_	12/12/07	Team member:	
Team member: _Nick Jones_	12/12/07	Team member:	

Transition Plan for *David*

Date: *12/12/07*

A transition is any major event that has an impact on a child and family, such as moving out of county or state, moving into or between programs, coming home from the NICU, changing a child care situation, or turning 3 years old. For children turning 3 years old, this page is to be filled out when they are 2 years and 3 months old.

What kind of transition is this? *Into program*

What does your family want and hope for your child for this transition? _____

Early intervention services

Date(s) of transition planning discussions: *will occur with each IFSP review*

Who participated in these discussions, and what options were discussed? _____

Parents and service coordinator participated in these discussions.

NEXT STEPS

Who will do what? When? *If David is still receiving early intervention services, the service cooordinator will help the family with referral and transition planning to Part B 90 days before his third birthday.*

If referring to public school system:

☐ Family given "Step Ahead at Age 3"
☐ Nonidentifying, confidential information forwarded to school district.
    Date:

☐ Transition planning conference held and preschool options discussed.
    Date: Comments: _____

☐ Referral made at least 90 days before third birthday
    Date: _____ Comments:

10

Chapter Appendix B

Individualized Education Program

SAMPLE

Child's name: *Stephanie Holmes*
Date of birth: *July 7, 2004*
Age: *4*

Street: *117 Maple Street*
City: *Centerville*
Zip: *00195*
Student ID#: *070-54-2133*
Medical alerts: *Seizure disorder*

Telephone: *014-223-2323*
County of residence: *Northern*
Male [ ]   Female [X]
Native language: *English*
Surrogate parent needed:
Yes [ ]   No [X]

Date of Committee on Preschool Special Education (CPSE)
   meeting:
Type of meeting:
   [ ] Initial   [ ] Requested review   [X] Annual review
   [ ] Reevaluation   [ ] _____
Date Individualized education program (IEP) is to be implemented:
09/15/08
Projected date of next review: *09/15/09*
Projected date of reevaluation meeting: *09/15/10*
More information:

Present Levels of Performance and Individual Needs

Current functioning and individual needs in consideration of

- The annual review of the IEP
- Consultation needs by related service personnel for classroom adaptations and physical accommodations

---

Academic/educational achievement and learning characteristics: Stephanie will attend her local elementary school and will be placed in the Friends Together preschool classroom. Her first psychological testing shows her functioning within the normal cognitive range. She will need consultation from related services of occupational therapy (OT) and physical therapy (PT) for physical adaptations in support of her learning.

Language and communication: Stephanie is very verbal and communicates well with her peers and adults.

Adaptive behavior: Stephanie is very independent in self-help skills. She has no difficulty eating. She wears a short brace (AFO) on one leg, but she is able to remove and put it on with little supervision. Infrequently she needs assistance with fastenings on her clothing. She is toilet trained, and her mother makes sure that she wears clothes that she can manage in the bathroom.

Cognitive: Psychological testing puts Stephanie well within the normal range.

Social development: Stephanie has many friends in the classroom. She tends to be a quiet observer, but she participates more as she gains confidence.

Socioemotional: She occasionally expresses some frustration when she is unable to complete a physical task due to the limited use of her left arm or her inability to keep up in gym. She and her friends are learning to be creative about adapting some of the physical tasks.

Behavior: Age appropriate; no concerns

Physical development: General growth and development are age appropriate. She is in the 25th percentile for height and weight.

Motor skills: Stephanie was diagnosed with cerebral palsy, left spastic hemiplegia, when she was 4 months old. Her motor skills are well developed on the right side. Her left arm is usually flexed, and her gait is uneven due to spasticity in the left leg.

Health: *Stephanie generally enjoys good health. She had a number of ear infections last year that prompted the pediatrician to order tubes placed in her ears.*

Management needs: *No concerns at this time.*

Measurable Annual Goals and Short-Term Instructional Objectives/Benchmarks

Annual goal: *Stephanie will increase her ability to improve use both arms and hands for bilateral activities.*

Instructional objectives or benchmarks	Evaluation		
	Criteria	Procedures	Schedule
Stephanie will use her left hand when appropriate to assist in writing and drawing activities.	*Stephanie will be able to write without her paper moving on the desk.*	*Reminders from teacher; OT/PT adaptations*	
Stephanie will use both arms and hands when carrying large objects, such as coats, clothing, books, and packages.	*Stephanie will need less assistance from peers and adults.*	*Reminders from teacher; OT/PT adaptations*	

Annual goal: *Stephanie will be able to use the playground with her peers.*

Instructional objectives or benchmarks	Evaluation		
	Criteria	Procedures	Schedule
Stephanie will be able to use the sliding pole with her friends.	*Stephanie can use the sliding pole as well as she would like to.*	*OT/PT adaptations*	
Stephanie will be able to play "Run, Sheep, Run" with her friends.	*Stephanie will play "Run, Sheep, Run" with her friends as successfully as she wants to.*	*OT/PT adaptations*	

Recommended Special Education Programs and Services

Special education program/services	Frequency	Duration	Location	Initiation date
Special class: *Not needed*				

Related services	Frequency	Duration	Location	Initiation date
OT consult	1x/month	50 min.	In classroom	9/15/08
PT consult	1x/month	50 min.	In classroom	9/15/08

Program modifications/ accommodations/supple- mentary aids and services	Frequency	Duration	Location	Initiation date
To be determined by teacher. OT as year progresses				

Assistive technology devices/services	Frequency	Duration	Location	Initiation date
None at this time. Refer if necessary for IT evaluation.				

Supports for school personnel on behalf of student	Frequency	Duration	Location	Initiation date
Seizure protocol	As needed	School year	Main office	9/15/08

Special transportation needs: Transportation to be provided.

Other preschool transportation needs:

Other:

The following testing accommodations will be used consistently
- In the student's education program
- In the administration of districtwide assessments of student achievement
- In the administration of state assessments of student achievement, consistent with state education department policy

Testing accommodation	Conditions	Specifications
None at this time		

PARTICIPATION IN ASSESSMENTS

[X] Student will participate in the same state or local assessments that are administered to students without disabilities.

[   ] The following state or local assessments (or part of an assessment) that are administered to preschool students without disabilities are not appropriate for the student:

Assessment(s): *Not applicable*

Reason not appropriate:

How student will be assessed:

PARTICIPATION WITH AGE-APPROPRIATE PEERS

Provision of special education services in a setting with no regular contact with age-appropriate peers without disabilities should only be considered when the nature or severity of the child's disability is such that education in a less restrictive environment with the use of supplementary aids and services cannot be satisfactorily achieved.

[   ] Explanation of the extent, if any, to which the student will not participate in appropriate activities with age-appropriate peers without disabilities

Will the preschool student receive services in a setting with no regular contact with age-appropriate peers without disabilities?   Yes [   ]   No [X]

Reporting Progress to Parents

The student's progress toward the annual goals and the extent to which the progress is sufficient to enable the student to achieve the goals will be reported to parents as follows.

Manner	Frequency
Conference with parents and team	*2x/year—October and April*

PLACEMENT RECOMMENDATION

10-month placement: *Local elementary school*

Approved preschool program provider: *Friends Together Preschool Classroom*

Extended school year eligible: Yes [ ]   No [*X*]
　　　　　　　　　　To be determined at next annual review
If yes, why:

Projected dates of services:　　/　　/　　to　　/　　/

Provider:

Site:

PARENT INFORMATION

Mother's/guardian's name: *Jonathan and Alice Holmes* Street: *117 Maple Street* City: *Centerville* ZIP: *00195*	Telephone: *014-223-2323* County of residence: *Northern* Native language of parent/guardian: *English* Interpreter needed for meeting: Yes [ ] No [*X*]
Father's/guardian's name: *See above* Street: City: ZIP: Surrogate parent needed: *No*	Telephone: County of residence: Native language of parent/guardian: Interpreter needed for meeting: Yes [ ] No [ ]
Surrogate parent's name: Street: City: ZIP:	Date appointed:　　/　　/ Telephone: Native language of surrogate parent: Interpreter needed for meeting: Yes [ ] No [ ]

STUDENT INFORMATION (For data collection purposes only)

Student's name: *Stephanie Holmes*

Race/ethnicity: *Caucasian*

CPSE participants		
Name	Professional title	CPSE member role
Edith West	*Assistant principal*	*Administrative representative*
Sandra Lane	*Teacher*	*Teacher*
Deborah Smith	*Occupational therapist*	*Related service provider*
Elise Kennedy (by report)	*Physical therapist*	*Related service provider*

11

Disruptive Behaviors

> **Key Concepts:** antecedent–behavior–consequence chart; social competence

One of the biggest challenges in group settings is disruptive behavior. When young children are together, conflicts are inevitable, and these conflicts often involve behaviors that challenge parents, teachers, and administrators. Two-year-olds may bite and pinch, three-year-olds may grab and push, and older preschoolers may try karate kicks and punches. Of course, most children are rarely physically aggressive. However, many people still think if a child has special needs, he or she will automatically be harder to manage in a group. But each child, with or without a disability, is different, so generalizations are impossible. This chapter provides a process to help program administrators analyze why a disruptive behavior occurs and develop a plan to address it.

Understanding Behavior

Behavior is a form of communication, so the first step is to figure out what a particular behavior means to a child. For example, Zack, age 3, throws himself on the floor when asked to leave circle time and wash his hands. The teacher reprimands him, and then the assistant teacher picks him up and tries to help him to the sink. Zack becomes increasingly upset and starts kicking and screaming. The director calls the parents; they meet and decide that Zack will have to sit out recess each time he has a tantrum. Zack misses recess and continues to have tantrums.

Everyone in this situation means well, but adults often try to find a solution before they fully understand the problem. In situations like these, the first thing to do is gather more information.

Collecting Information and Analyzing the Behavior

To understand Zack's behavior, we need to know more about Zack. How is he doing developmentally? Are there any medical concerns? Next, we need to know about the environment. Are other children having trouble with moving from circle time to hand washing? Have there been any changes in the staff or children in the classroom? It's also helpful to talk with the family. Do they see this behavior at home?

Now we need more information about Zack's tantrums. Do they happen every day? When did they start? It's often helpful to systematically collect information about the tantrums by recording when and how often the tantrums occur as well as what happens right before and right after each outburst on an **antecedent–behavior–consequence chart** (see Figure 11.1 for an example of Zack's collected information). We also need to understand what Zack is trying to communicate through his meltdowns. Does he not want to leave circle time? Does he not like to wash his hands? Is he having trouble with other transitions? Is he easily overwhelmed by noise and movement? Does he not understand what is expected of him? Finally, we need to look at what happens when Zack has a tantrum. Does he get more adult attention? Does he avoid something he doesn't like?

Developing a Hypothesis

When all of the information is collected, it is easier to make a guess about what the behavior means. In this case, it turns out that Zack has trouble with many transitions both at school and at home. He has a hard time leaving an activity he enjoys and frequently protests by throwing himself on the floor and yelling. He digs in his heels when urged to hurry up and becomes increasingly upset. The end result is that he gets a lot of adult attention and is carried to the next activity. Once he is involved in the new activity, he usually enjoys it. Interestingly, Zack has more tantrums right before lunch and again late in the afternoon, so hunger and fatigue may be factors.

Identifying a Target Behavior

Because Zack is disrupting the whole class, it's natural to want to find an immediate solution. Unfortunately, changing a disruptive behavior takes

ACTIVITY	ANTECEDENT	BEHAVIOR	CONSEQUENCE
Morning Circle—Monday	The teacher sends five children to go wash their hands before snack. Zack waits. The teacher then asks Zack to go wash his hands. The teacher repeats her direction and tells Zack to stop fussing and hurry up because other children are waiting.	Zack looks at the teacher, whines, and lies down on the floor. He then starts to kick his feet and yell.	The teaching assistant comes over, tries to pick Zack up, and leads him to the sink.
Morning Circle—Tuesday	The teacher sends 10 children to go wash their hands before snack. Zack sits next to the teacher and watches. The teacher tells Zack to go wash his hands. The teacher repeats her direction and tells Zack he'll miss snack if he doesn't hurry up.	Zack throws himself on the floor and kicks his feet. When the teacher reminds him to hurry up, he starts yelling.	The teacher ignores him and goes over to the snack table. The assistant comes over and tries to pick Zack up. He goes limp and continues to protest.
Morning Circle—Wednesday	The teacher sends Zack and his friend Andrew first to go wash their hands.	Andrew takes Zack's hand, and they walk over to the sink.	The teacher and the assistant don't say anything to Zack or Andrew.

Figure 11.1. Antecedent–behavior–consequence chart for Zack.

time, and it's important to start with a very specific goal. For example, with Zack, we would start with one transition—moving from circle time to hand washing. The goal is for Zack to leave circle time and go wash his hands with only two reminders from the teacher.

Developing a Behavior Intervention Plan

When we're trying to change disruptive behavior in young children, we need to first look at the environment and the expectations of the adults involved. Parents and teachers often try to motivate a child by establishing a system of rewards and punishments. This can be an important component of a plan, but it has to be part of a more comprehensive approach.

Involving the Child

Before making any changes, the teacher talked to Zack about what was going to happen. She told him that everyone wanted him to be happy in class, and when he kicked and yelled it was not fun for him or for anyone else. She said she was going to use a special signal when she wanted Zack to leave circle time and wash his hands. They decided she would wiggle her nose as a reminder.

For Zack, changing the circle routine was very important. With 15 children in the group, he had been one of the last children to leave circle time. After looking at the data, the teacher had Zack and his best friend leave the circle first and go straight to the instructional assistant to wash his hands. She stopped reminding and reprimanding him and instead just pointed towards the sink and then wiggled her nose. Meanwhile, the assistant was waiting at the sink and holding out the soap bottle to Zack. After Zack washed his hands, he got to sit at the snack table and immediately have a cracker.

Involving the Family

Zack's family was also involved. His mother made him a picture book about leaving circle time and washing hands. It had a picture of Zack at each step of the process and ended with one of him smiling at the sink. She read this book to Zack each morning when she dropped him off.

Involving the Staff

Finally, because hunger was probably making the transition harder, the assistant took Zack aside and gave him one or two apple slices right before circle time started. The teacher continued to chart the frequency of

Zack's meltdowns. Zack's daily tantrums at circle decreased to only once a twice or week and became much shorter and less intense. The teacher then started to use a similar technique with other transition times.

Role of the Administrator

It's much easier to manage challenging situations when you have a process in place to help analyze each situation and develop a plan. This approach works for children with or without special needs and helps bring everyone together to find a solution.

As the director, you can put a process like this in place and support the staff and family as they move through it. There will be occasions when solutions are not so easy and you may need to bring in additional expertise.

Serious and Persistent Behaviors

Some children have more serious and persistent behaviors that interfere with their ability to pay attention to the classroom activities. Examples of these behaviors are self-stimulatory behaviors, such as rocking, hand flapping, and teeth grinding. There are other behaviors that endanger the children themselves or others. These self-injurious behaviors include head banging, eye poking, and biting one's arms. These behaviors are quite difficult to handle. Occasionally, you may have children with severe emotional problems who can be extremely aggressive or destructive.

Some of these serious behaviors are caused by physiological needs in the child (National Institute of Neurological Disorders and Stroke, n.d.). Eye poking is often seen in children who are blind. These children may experience some visual stimuli from the pressure in an ordinarily deprived sense. Children who have metabolic disorders, such as Lesch-Nyhan syndrome, engage in self-injurious behavior as a result of their organic dysfunction (Kurtz et al., 2003). It is almost impossible to completely stop behaviors from organic causes. It is also very difficult to understand what the child is trying to communicate because these behaviors often occur in children who are nonverbal. If the child becomes upset or angry, you may see an increase in these behaviors.

In such cases, it is important to consider the following questions:

- Is the child or others at risk for injury?

- Does the behavior interfere with learning and socialization?

- Does the behavior interfere with the learning of others by distracting or upsetting them?

- How often does this specific behavior happen?

- In what situations or settings does the behavior occur?

- How intense is the behavior? Does it look worse than it is? Is gentle pressure being applied, or is actual damage taking place?

- How long does the behavior last? Has it been happening for a long time? Do you expect it to continue, or is it related to a specific activity or event? For example, is the child under stress as a result of illness or problems at home?

When such behaviors occur, it is important to get assistance in handling them. These behaviors can be very hard to change. Ask the parents what they do and what they feel is appropriate for you to do in your program. If the child has a special behavior program, ask to see the plan and get help to learn how to use it. If the child has a behavior specialist working with her, ask if that person can consult with your program or seek a specialist to help you in your program. Do not try to take on this task alone. Your first responsibility is to the well-being of the children and staff.

Crisis Management

Once in a while you may encounter a situation where children are in immediate danger. The following are some crisis management techniques you can teach your staff to use.

1. *Stop the aggression.* An adult intervenes and stops the aggressive or destructive behavior. The adult then separates the children if more than one child is involved.

2. *Remove the disruptive child.* An adult removes the disruptive child and directs the child to a certain chair, quiet corner, or an out-of-the-way place.

3. *Attend to the hurt child.* An adult praises the hurt child for remaining calm, following rules, and focusing on work and play.

4. *Calmly restate the expectations to the disruptive child.* An adult must be briefly state the desired behavior. This is not a time for teaching or discussing. Use simple direct language, such as, "There is no hitting," not "How many times have I told you not to hit? It hurts and makes the other children cry, and I get mad." Tell the child how you want him or her to behave. Direct the child's attention to the rules and use visual cues if it helps the child to understand.

5. *Allow "get yourself together" time.* An adult helps the disruptive child to relax. If it helps, model the following "relaxation" strategies:

- Take a few deep breaths

- Move your shoulders up and then down

- Stop and wait, or stop and think

- Take a short walk in the hallway

- Squeeze your hands

- Stamp your feet

- Relax your muscles—be a rag doll

- Say something to yourself, or slowly count to five to yourself

6. *Support the disruptive child.* An adult supports the child when he or she re-enters the classroom activity and stays with the child until he or she is engaged in constructive activity.

7. *Choose a calming activity,* such as the listening center. Following the routine and completing the interrupted activity may calm the child.

Prosocial Strategies

Social interaction is one of the most complex set of skills that a young child learns. It requires the integration of cognitive, language, and motor skills. An infant develops his first relationship with his parents or primary caregiver. This early attachment sets the pattern for future development of relationships and social skills. The continuous interaction of how a child behaves toward other people and how those people behave toward him or her are indicators of **social competence** (i.e., the ability to achieve social goals successfully). Social competence includes prosocial skills, such as caring for others, empathizing, helping, cooperating, and making friends. You can enhance the development of these skills by selecting and implementing a curriculum that fosters these skills.

One of the most common reasons that parents want an inclusive setting for their children is because they want them to be part of their neighborhood and to have friends. Parents want their children to develop good social skills. Children with developmental delays may have difficulty making and keeping friends. The place to develop these skills is in regular settings with other children. Being around peers is an important factor but physical proximity alone is not enough. As the administrator, you can use specific strategies, such as those listed below, to promote social relationships and prosocial behavior in children with and without disabilities.

1. Organize play sessions by grouping socially competent children with those who are less socially skilled.

2. Plan activities to help children develop alternative solutions to difficult social situations.

3. Assign an adult mediator to guide the conflict resolution.

4. Help children to learn to recognize that "help and cooperation" are appropriate in social situations. Point out and create helping situations for the children.

5. Help children to observe a play group they wish to enter, figure out the group's theme and purpose, and help them think of a role they could play or something they could contribute to the group. Teach children how to ask to be part of a group and how to join or be included in the play.

6. Help facilitate conversations that contribute to the maintenance of cohesive play.

7. Help children recognize, read, and respond to others' emotional cues.

8. Help the peer groups to understand a disliked child's behavior, but do not force peers to play with that child.

9. Suggest ways for the family to supplement and support the child's social acceptance, such as having a friend over after school.

Shadows and One-to-One Assistants

Occasionally, a child with special needs may require extra adult time and attention to manage the classroom routines. In these situations, it is not uncommon for a parent or classroom teacher to ask for an individual assistant. The reasoning is that the individual assistant, often referred to as a shadow, will be able to help the child participate in classroom routines. Clearly, some children with special needs require individual attention, but so do most children at some point during the day. Before deciding that a child needs a shadow, think about other ways to reduce the adult to child ratio in the classroom so that every child will benefit. Also, when one adult shadows one child, it can result in increased isolation for that child because the other children may perceive her as unavailable as a play partner.

The beginning of the school year is challenging for all the children and adults. Everyone needs to get to know each other and learn the routines. A child with special needs who requires a lot of individual attention during the first weeks of school may become increasingly independent as he becomes accustomed to the routines. Consider arranging for a student teacher, college intern, floating assistant, or volunteer to provide support to the entire classroom for the first month of school. If a child comes with a personal assistant, ask if that person may spend time with other children in the group as well. If you can find a way to reduce the adult–child ratio, the teacher will be able to spend more time with any child needing extra attention.

Conclusion

Disruptive behaviors are upsetting to everyone involved, the child, the family, and the staff. Developing and implementing a systematic process to analyze the situation; involve the child, family, and staff; and consider changes in the environment, routines, and behaviors of the adults will give you a consistent way to manage these difficult situations. Remember, your goal is not just to stop the undesired behavior but to teach the child a new way of coping.

12

Health and Safety Services
in Early Childhood Programs

Key Concepts: infectious disease

The licensing regulations of early childhood programs serve to protect children from harm and promote their healthy development. It is important for early childhood administrators to become knowledgeable about all applicable regulations. Your policies must continue to be enforced, updated, and reviewed at least annually to minimize the spread of illnesses and communicable diseases and ensure safety.

Know the Child Care Regulations in Your State

Most states have regulations for the following health policies:

- Immunizing children

- Administering and storing medications

- Maintaining medical records

- Knowing health-related admission procedures, isolating children who are ill, and returning to the early childhood program after illness

- Notifying parents concerning outbreaks of communicable diseases

Thanks to Janeen McCracken Taylor, Ph.D., who provided the original health information in the first edition.

- Reporting diseases

- Hand washing and diapering

Early childhood programs should have written health practice policies that include clear statements regarding each of the previous areas. Policies should also describe how to implement each practice and how to ensure that the implementation is correct. Give these policies to staff and families. Simplified versions of important health-related policies should appear in the parent handbook.

Promoting Good Health Practices

All staff in early childhood programs need to be aware of the applicable state regulations and the Occupational Safety and Health Administration (OSHA) requirements. Many states require that all staff have first aid and CPR training annually. In addition, staff training should address and promote good health practices related to hand washing; using barriers, such as gloves and smocks; handling food properly; cleaning up bodily fluid (e.g., urine, feces, vomit, blood) spills; and diapering and toilet training.

Hand Washing

Hand washing is the most important action we can take to lower the risk of catching or transmitting an **infectious disease** (Kotch et al., 2007). Hand washing should become routine throughout the day. Display illustrations of thorough hand washing prominently near every sink to remind children and staff to wash their hands often and carefully.

For proper hand washing, use liquid soap, a lot of running water, and plenty of brisk hand rubbing to scrub all surfaces of your hands and lower arms for a minimum of 10 seconds. One technique is to scrub for the amount of time it takes to sing simple songs, such as "Yankee Doodle" or "Pop Goes the Weasel." This will ensure enough time for a thorough cleaning of your hands and model a desirable behavior for the children in your care. After rinsing with running water, use paper towels to dry your hands.

Cloth towels and bar soaps are less desirable than disposable towels and liquid soap because they can harbor germs. It is preferable to have liquid soap and disposable towels in the bathroom of your classroom (see Figure 12.1 of an example of a bathroom accommodated with liquid soap). Sinks equipped with knee or foot pedals are preferable to hand-operated faucets to avoid contamination from handles. If knee or foot pedals are not feasible, then you can turn off faucets using paper towels as a barrier. For additional protection, spray faucet handles with

Figure 12.1. Example of a bathroom sink with liquid soap and step accommodations.

disinfectant after each use, but make sure the disinfectant is stored out of children's reach. Skin can become dry and chapped when hands are washed as frequently as recommended. Liberal use of creams and lotions can minimize skin problems. Good hygiene can reduce the risk of staff and children getting sick.

Using Gloves and Special Clothing

Using barriers, such as gloves or smocks, is another method to protect against illness and infections. Staff should use gloves for diaper changing, wound care, or bodily spill clean ups. Fit and thickness are important. Gloves that are too large make tasks more difficult. If the gloves are too small, then there is risk of perforation or tearing. If gloves are too thin, then they may not provide enough protection. Staff may also want to wear aprons or smocks to protect clothing and act as a barrier to germs. Protective garments should be laundered daily with hot, soapy water.

Handling Food Properly

All food handling procedures of the licensing agency should be followed strictly. In some states, staff are required to attend food handlers training. Always wash your hands before handling food and feeding children. If staff dispense meals, then servers should wear gloves. Children should be supervised so that there is no sharing of food from plate to plate.

Another important aspect of food handling is storing food, refrigerating perishables, and cleaning up after meals or snacks. Special care should be taken with food and formula for infants and toddlers.

Handling Bodily Fluid Spills

When a child is injured or becomes ill, first comfort the child. Teach older children to use their own hands to cover a scrape or cut and to let staff know about it right away. Next, get the emergency cleanup kit, which contains several pairs of latex gloves, paper towels, disinfectant, and plastic bags.

For the cleanup, it is best to use universal precautions, which are measures taken when there may be contact with bodily fluids (Centers for Disease Control and Prevention, 1987, 1996). The American Academy of Pediatrics (2002, 2004, 2005) suggested using universal precautions when there is a high risk of spreading infection through direct contact or high-risk caregiving procedures. It makes sense to be cautious with all children because some illnesses can be spread even when there are no symptoms. Use the following universal precautions when cleaning up bodily fluid spills.

- Wear a new pair of disposable gloves for each incident or child.

- Blot the spill with paper towels to reduce the amount of liquid or contaminated material.

- Dispose of all contaminated material (e.g., soiled paper towels) in a doubled plastic bag that is clearly marked "Caution: Contaminated Materials."

- Remove gloves and dispose of them in the same bag.

- Seal and dispose of the bag (check with the local health department regarding disposal regulations).

- Put on new gloves to clean the spill area with a solution containing one part household bleach to 10 parts water (this must be made fresh daily) or the approved disinfectant for your program.

- Put on a new pair of gloves to clean remaining fluids.

- Carefully remove the gloves for disposal. Latex gloves provide a barrier to germs and prevent contamination through direct contact with infectious material.

Have the approved disinfectant or bleach solution readily available in a pump spray bottle for application to small or hard-to-reach surfaces.

Washed surfaces can be left to air dry or after 20 minutes can be rinsed with clean water and then left to air dry. Disinfection should follow all bodily fluid spills. Bottles and storage containers of disinfectant, bleach, or bleach solutions should be clearly labeled and sealed with child-resistant caps and kept out of a child's reach.

Plan to provide staff training every year on preventing the spread of infectious diseases and cleaning up bodily fluid spills. Conducting a simulation is one way to get everyone involved. You can use dolls, so everyone has a chance to practice diapering techniques, and instant oatmeal is a good, but messy, stand-in for practicing bodily fluid spill cleanup. Staff can work in pairs to help each other follow the required procedures.

Diapering and Toileting Techniques

Because diaper changing can involve contact with feces or urine, both of which can contain infectious matter, it carries the risk of contamination for the child, caregiver, or environment. Use gloves on both hands for diaper changing, cleanup procedures, and toileting assistance. Even though diaper changing may seem like a one-handed job, you never know when you might suddenly need to use both hands. Clean gloves should be used for each child, and diaper changing should be confined to designated areas separate from food preparation and serving areas (see Figure 12.2 for an example of a designated diaper area).

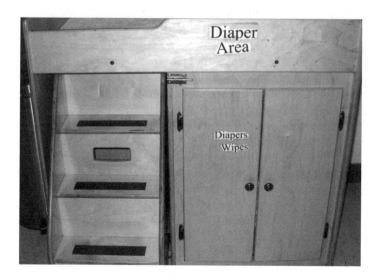

Figure 12.2.   Example of a designated diaper area.

Diaper-changing areas or tables should have washable surfaces and be located near a sink. Place a new disposable covering under each child, and discard it after one use. Put soiled diapers and wipes in plastic bags, and discard in a plastic-lined trash container that has a foot pedal to open the lid. Trash cans should have tightly fitted lids and should be kept out of the reach of children (e.g., on the outside of the door, on a tall shelf). Also, place soiled clothing in plastic bags, seal them, and store in a covered container until they are picked up by the parents. Wash and disinfect the changing surface after every procedure. Finally, before returning to other activities, you and the child, as appropriate, should wash your hands carefully, even if you wear gloves during diaper changing.

Health Policies

Litigation under the ADA related to health issues had prompted the creation of new policies for implementation in early childhood programs. The Department of Justice has included clear examples of policies in settlements that are posted on the ADA website. As with any personal information pertaining to families, programs must ensure that confidentiality is maintained.

Confidentiality

Most states have clear regulatory requirements regarding confidentiality. For example, if a child in your program has a communicable disease (e.g., hepatitis A, HIV) or a health condition, then you may not disclose that to other families. You also have an obligation, however, to provide a safe and healthy environment for all children attending the program.

Even vigilant efforts will not prevent all illness. If an outbreak occurs, then parents should be notified promptly while maintaining the confidentiality of the child who is infected. It is imperative that other families receive information regarding the possibility of infection. To avoid a breach of confidentiality, a general letter containing a description of the illness should be sent to all families of children enrolled at the program. The letter should include information about the illness, its characteristics, the ways it is transmitted, likelihood of infection, and precautionary or treatment measures. You can collect information on common infectious diseases in advance so that they will be on hand in the event of an outbreak.

Policy Changes Prompted by
Americans with Disabilities Act Case Law

Several cases about health conditions have been brought before the circuit courts. These cases address allergies, asthma, diabetes, viral infections (e.g., hepatitis, HIV, AIDS), and seizures. All of the cases have been settled, and the courts have required early childhood programs to make specific modifications in policies and procedures.

The courts have upheld that children with these health-related conditions qualify as individuals with disabilities. Early childhood programs have been asked to write a nondiscrimination statement that prohibits discrimination against children with disabilities. In addition, programs must put a plan in place to make reasonable modifications for the children. For example, the courts required programs to find information on the health condition and to train staff on the care needed. Programs were required to create forms to gather information about the needs of the children and to develop procedures to provide care and manage emergencies. Whether a child has a disability, it is good practice to have pertinent information on all children in case of an emergency and during times of acute illness. Table 12.1 shows the types of special health care needs that have been addressed through litigation and the required accommodations.

Table 12.1. Types of special health care needs addressed through litigation and the required accommodations

Health condition	Required modification
Allergies	Development of policies and procedures for treatment of severe allergies; waiver for administering emergency treatment (use of EpiPen); staff training
Asthma	Development of policies for management of asthma and the administration of medications; request for authorization for treatment (medications, inhaler, nebulizer); waiver for administering medical treatment; staff training
Diabetes	Development of policies and procedures for diabetes management; administering blood sugar testing; staff training for recognition of when to administer treatment; waiver for emergency treatment
Seizure disorders	Development of policies and procedures for seizure management; waiver for emergency treatment
Viral infections (e.g., HIV, AIDS, hepatitis)	Development and enforcement of policies and procedures using universal hygiene procedures; no special care; staff training on preventing spread of communicable diseases

The settlements and summary judgments of these cases are on the U.S. Department of Justice, ADA web site with some of the nondiscrimination statements and document samples. The courts found that none of these conditions posed a direct threat to the child, staff, or other children or warranted exclusion from an early childhood program.

The American Academy of Pediatrics has published several excellent resources to provide guidance for health and safety in early childhood programs. There are also web sites that provide information and guidelines to families and professionals promoting good health (see the resource list in Appendix B in the back of this book).

Summary

Health and safety practices in early childhood programs are two of the most critical components to define, monitor, and enforce to protect the health and well-being of the staff, children and families of your program. Each administrator must ensure that policies are comprehensive, up to date, and reviewed annually.

References

Alvarez v. Fountainhead, Inc., 55 F. Supp. 2d 1048 (N.D. Cal. 1999).

American Academy of Pediatrics. (2002). *National health and safety performance standards: Guidelines for out-of-home child care programs* (2nd ed.).
Elk Grove, IL: Author.

American Academy of Pediatrics. (2004). *Managing infectious diseases in child
care and schools: A quick reference guide.* Elk Grove Village, IL: Author.

American Academy of Pediatrics. (2005). *Health in child care manual* (4th ed.).
Elk Grove, IL: Author.

Americans with Disabilities Act Accessibility Guidelines (ADAAG) for Buildings,
Facilities, and Play Areas, 34 C.F.R. § 1191 (2000).

Americans with Disabilities Act of 1990, 42 U.S.C. §§ 12101 *et seq.*

Architectural and Transportation Barriers Compliance Board. (2004). *The Americans with Disabilities Act–accessibility guidelines.* Washington, DC: Author.

Breen v. State of Connecticut, Department of Public Health and Addiction Services, CV94-0535185 S. WL 62174 (Conn. Sup. Ct. 1994).

Burriola v. Greater Toledo YMCA, 133 F. Supp. 2d 1034 (N.D. Ohio 2001).

Centers for Disease Control and Prevention. (1987). *Fact sheet: Universal precautions for prevention of HIV and other blood borne pathogens.* Atlanta, GA:
U.S. Department of Health and Human Services.

Centers for Disease Control and Prevention. (1996). *Fact sheet: Universal precautions for prevention of HIV and other blood-borne pathogens.* Atlanta, GA:
U.S. Department of Health and Human Services.

Child Care Bureau. (1995). *Passages to inclusion.* Leadership forum. Washington, DC: U.S. Department of Human Services.

Child Care Law Center. (1997). *Americans with Disabilities Act and child care
litigation updates.* San Francisco: Child Care Law Center.

Civil Rights Division. (1993a). *Title II technical assistance.* Washington, DC: U.S.
Department of Justice.

Civil Rights Division. (1993b). *Title III technical assistance.* Washington, DC:
U.S. Department of Justice.

Doggett, L., & George, J. (1993). *All kids count.* Arlington, TX: The Arc.

Education of the Handicapped Act Amendments of 1986, PL 99-457, 20 U.S.C. §§
1400 *et seq.*

E.M. v. Town Sports International, Inc., and TSI Wellesley, Inc., C.A. No. 05-10611-GAO (2006).

Enforcing the Americans with Disabilities Act, Part 2. (n.d.). Retrieved May 22, 2008, from http://www.ada.gov/5yearadarpt/ii_enforcing_pt2.htm

Freedom of Information Act of 1966, PL 85-619, 5 U.S.C. §§ 552 *et seq.*

Gil de Larmadrid, M. (1996). Child care and the ADA: Litigation updates. *Exceptional Parent, 26*(2), 40–43.

Great Lakes Resource Access Project. (1992–1993). The Americans with Disabilities Act and Head Start: Practical strategies for developing compliance plans. *Quarterly Resource, 7*(1), 1–15.

Harms, T., Clifford, R.M., & Cryer, D. (2003). *Infant/Toddler Environmental Rating Scale–Revised.* New York: Teachers College Press.

Hyson, M.C. (Ed.). (1998). Inclusion in early childhood settings. *Early Childhood Research Quarterly, 13*(1).

Individuals with Disabilities Education Act (IDEA) Amendments of 1991, 20 U.S.C. §§ 1400 *et seq.*

Individuals with Disabilities Education Act (IDEA) Amendments of 1997, 20 U.S.C. §§ 1400 *et seq.*

Individuals with Disabilities Education Act (IDEA) of 1990, 20 U.S.C. §§ 1400 *et seq.*

Individuals with Disabilities Education Improvement Act (IDEA) of 2004, 20 U.S.C. §§ 1400 *et seq.*

Ireland v. Kansas District of the Wesleyan Church, Civ. A. No. 94-4077-DES. WL 413807 (D. Kan. 1994).

J.H. v. ABC Care, Inc., 953 F. Supp. 675 (D. MD 1996).

Kotch, J. B., Isbell, P., Weber, D. J., Nguyen, V., Savage, E., et al. (2007). Hand washing and diapering equipment reduces disease in children in out-of-home child care center. *Pediatrics, 120*(1), e29–e36.

Kurtz, P.F., Chin, M.D., Huete, J.M., Tarbox, R.S.F., O'Connor, J.T., Paclawski, T.R., et al. (2003). Functional analysis and treatment of self-injurious behavior in young children: A summary of 30 cases. *Journal of Applied Behavior Analysis, 36*, 205–219.

Land v. Baptist Medical Center, No. 98-2019EA (8th dist. 1999).

National Association for the Education of Young Children (NAEYC). (2006). *Early childhood program standards and accreditation criteria.* Washington, DC: Author.

National Council on Disability. (1997). *Equality of opportunity: The making of the Americans with Disabilities Act.* Washington, DC: Author.

National Institute of Neurological Disorders and Stroke. (n.d.) *Lesch-Nyhan Syndrome information page.* Retrieved May 27, 2008, from http://www.ninds.nih.gov/disorders/lesch_nyhan/lesch_nyhan.htm

No Child Left Behind Act of 2001, PL 107-110, 115 Stat. 1425, 20 U.S.C. §§ 6301 *et seq.*

Orr v. KinderCare Learning Centers, Inc., No. CV-S-95-507 (E.D. Cal. 1995).

Osborne, A.G., & Dimattia, P. (1994). The Individuals with Disabilities Education Act's least restrictive environment mandate: Legal implication. *Exceptional Children, 61*(1), 6–14.

Pennsylvania Association of Retarded Citizens (PARC) v. Commonwealth, 334 F. Supp. 1257.

Rehabilitation Act of 1973, PL 93-112, 29 U.S.C. §§ 701 *et seq.*

Richey, D.D., Richey, L.H., & Webb, J. (1996). Inclusive infant–toddler groups: Strategies for success. *Dimensions of Early Childhood, 24*(4), 10–16.

Roberts v. KinderCare Learning Centers, Inc. No. 86 F.3d 844, 847 (D. Minn. 1995).

Roberts v. KinderCare Learning Centers, Inc. No. 95-3423 86 F. 3d 844 (8th Cir. 1996).

Stainback, S., & Stainback, W. (1996). *Inclusion: A guide for educators.* Baltimore: Paul H. Brookes Publishing Co.

State of the Art, Inc. (Producer). (1994). *Regular lives.* PBS Video.

Stuthard v. KinderCare Learning Centers, Inc., No. C2-96-0185 (D. Ohio. Feb. 26, 1996).

Talan, T.N., & Bloom, P.J. (2004). *Program administration scale.* New York: Teachers College Press.

U.S. Department of Justice. (1993). *The Americans with Disabilities Act: Title III technical assistance manual with yearly supplements.* Washington, DC: Author.

U.S. Department of Justice. (2000). *Enforcing the Americans with Disabilities Act: Looking back on a decade of progress.* Retrieved July 3, 2000, from http://www.doj.gov/crt/ada/pubs/10thrpt.htm

U.S. Department of Justice. (2003). *Enforcing the Americans with Disabilities Act: Status report.* Retrieved May 23, 2008, from http://www.ada.gov/janmar04.htm

U.S. Department of Justice. (2006). *Access for all: Five years of progress.* Retrieved March 8, 2007, from http://www.doj.gov/crt/ada

U.S. v. ABC Nursery, Inc., No. 97-C-441 (W.D. Wis. 1997).

U.S. v. Happy Time Day Care Center, 6 F. Supp. ed at 1081 (W.D. Wis. 1997).

U.S. v. Kiddie Ranch, Happy Time, and ABC Playhouse, No. 97-C-440 (W.D. Wis. 1997).

U.S. v. Smyrna Playschool, Inc., No. 202-19-46 (1998).

Wolery, M., Holcombe, A., Brookfield, J., Huffman, K., Schroeder, C., Martin, et al. (1993a). The extent and nature of preschool mainstreaming: A survey of general educators. *Journal of Special Education, 27*(2), 222–234.

Wolery, M., Holcombe, A., Venn, M.L., Brookfield, J., Huffman, K., Schroeder, C., et al. (1993b). Mainstreaming in early childhood programs: Current status and relevant issues. *Young Children, 49*(1), 78–84.

A

Glossary

accommodation An effort to structure or manipulate the environment so that an individual with a disability can experience the social or physical environment in a meaningful way.

accommodation plan A plan documenting how the accommodations needed to meet the needs of individuals with disabilities will be acquired and implemented.

antecedent–behavior–consequence chart When evaluating a child with difficult-to-manage behavior, this chart describes the situation before the behavior occurs, describes the behavior, and describes what happened after the behavior occurred. Such descriptions should include who was present and the actions of each child and adult. Observations should be clearly separated from interpretations.

auxiliary aid or service 1) Qualified interpreter or other effective method of making aurally delivered materials available to individuals with hearing impairments; 2) qualified reader, taped text, or other effective method of making visually delivered materials available to individuals with visual impairments; 3) acquisition or modification of equipment or devices; and 4) other similar service and action.

barrier free Referring to programs or facilities accessible to individuals with disabilities.

Child Find The screening and evaluation service provided by local school systems to assist in identifying young children that are in need of special education services.

chronological placement Placement of children in a classroom determined by age.

communicable disease   *See* infectious disease.

direct threat   A significant risk to the health or safety of others that cannot be eliminated by a modification of policies, practices, or procedures or by the provision of auxiliary aids or services.

disability   A 1) physical or mental impairment that substantially limits one or more major life activities of such an individual, 2) a record of such an impairment, or 3) being regarded as having an impairment.

discrimination   Denial of benefits of rights, services, programs, or activities.

dual placement   Children enrolled in both a special education program and in an early childhood program concurrently.

due process procedure   A procedure that safeguards the rights of children with disabilities and their families under the Individuals with Disabilities Education Act (IDEA) of 1990 (PL 101-476) and its amendments.

eligibility   A determination that a child fits one of the disability categories under the Individuals with Disabilities Education Act (IDEA) of 1990 (PL 101-476) and its amendments and may receive special education services.

eligibility criteria   Those requirements imposed by a child care programs to determine admission to the program.

essential function   A critical job-related duty in a job description that must be carried out by the employee.

full participation   The opportunity for an individual with a disability to benefit from or participate in any goods or services offered by a program.

fundamental alteration   A change in the basic nature of the services offered by a program. A program does not need to change the nature or mix of goods that it typically offers to the public to allow accessibility by an individual with a disability. For example, a bookstore must be physically accessible to individuals with disabilities, but it is not required to stock large print or braille books.

individual with a disability   An individual with a physical or mental impairment that substantially limits one or more major life activities of such individual or an individual who has a record of such an impairment or who is regarded as having an impairment.

inclusion   The philosophy that all children have the right to be included with their peers in all age-appropriate activities throughout life.

infectious disease   An illness that can be transmitted; *also called* communicable disease.

integrated setting   A setting in which individuals with and without disabilities fully participate together.

integration   Pertaining to specifically designed programs to combine typical children and children with disabilities.

learning plan   A plan that documents the specific learning goals, outcomes, and activities for a child with a disability. It also includes the supports needed and a timeline for the achievement of the goals.

least restrictive environment (LRE)   Terminology from the Individuals with Disabilities Education Act (IDEA) of 1990 (PL 101-476) and its amendments that states that children with disabilities should be educated in an environment that is not more restrictive than they need.

major life activity   An activity that is necessary for caring for oneself, such as performing manual tasks, walking, seeing, hearing, speaking, breathing, learning, or working.

multi-age grouping   A group of children of more than one age who are combined for developmental programming.

natural environment   A location or situation in which a child with a disability would be participating had the child not had a disability (e.g., general education instead of special education).

nondiscrimination policy   A policy stating that a program will not discriminate and also delineates that specific criteria will not be used for discrimination.

nonessential function   A job-related function that is included in a job description, but is not considered critical or required for hiring.

person-first language   The use of descriptors that indicate the individual rather than the disability designation (e.g., *a person with a disability* rather than *a disabled person*).

physical accessibility   The availability and usability of a site, building, or portion of building by individuals with disabilities. A facility is physically accessible when it adheres to the Uniform Federal Accessibility Standards (UFAS) or Americans with Disabilities Act Accessibility Guidelines (ADAAG) by removing architectural and communication barriers that are structural.

occupational therapy   Services that help a child in fine motor, oral-motor, perceptual/motor, sensory processing, and daily living activities.

physical therapy   Services that help a child develop and use motor skills related to coordination, balance, muscle strength, endurance, range of motion and mobility.

program review   An administrative review to ensure that program components are in place and may be used for evaluative purposes.

public accommodation   A facility, operated by a private entity, whose operations affect commerce (e.g., nursery, elementary, secondary, undergraduate, or postgraduate private school), other place of education, or a child care center.

public entity   Any state or local government; any department, agency, special purpose district, or other instrumentality of a state or states or local government.

qualified individual with a disability   An individual with a disability who, with or without reasonable accommodation, can perform the essential functions of the employment position that such individual holds or desires.

readily achievable   Easily accomplished without much difficulty or expense.

reasonable modification   A modification in policies, practices, or procedures necessary to afford such goods, services, facilities, privileges, advantages, or accommodations to individuals with disabilities, unless the entity can demonstrate that making such modifications would fundamentally alter the nature of such goods, services, facilities, privileges, advantages, or accommodations.

related service   A transportation or other developmental, corrective, and support service required to assist a child with a disability to benefit from special education.

religious entity   An entity that is provided financial and administrative support by a religious organization.

social competence   The emotional, social, and cognitive skills and behaviors a child needs to develop successful social adaptation.

speech therapy   Services provided by a speech-language pathologist who specializes in communication disorders such as voice quality, pronunciation (articulation), oral-motor skills, vocabulary (language), and hearing.

special education   Specially designed instruction for a qualifying child with a disability, provided at no cost to parents, that meets their child's unique needs.

team teaching   A method of developing a program for a child that uses information and combined efforts of all service providers.

undue burden   Significant difficulty or expense.

undue hardship   An action requiring significant difficulty or expense.

B

Resources

This resource section provides additional information related to the Americans with Disabilities Act (ADA) of 1990 (PL 101-336), disability laws, and inclusive programming. The comments following some resources are descriptions and should not be taken as an endorsement.

WEB SITES

American Academy of Pediatrics

http://www.aap.org

This web site has a parenting corner and specific written resources.

The Americans with Disabilities Act Home Page

http://www.usdoj.gov/crt/ada

This web site is the most comprehensive location for all information pertaining to the ADA.

Architectural and Transportation Barriers Compliance Board

http://www.access-board.gov

This web site is the leading resource on accessible design and can provide ADA Accessibility Guidelines and information about accessibility in children's facilities.

Child Care Law Center

http://www.childcarelaw.org

This web site has written materials about the ADA directed to child care participants.

Federal Communications Commission

http://www.fcc.gov

This web site provides information about telecommunication and relay services and numbers for state contacts about telecommunication services for the disabled.

Healthy Kids, Healthy Care:
Parents as Partners in Promoting Healthy and Safe Child Care

http://www.healthykids.us

This web site was created by the National Resource Center for Health and Safety in Child Care and Early Education. It provides information for parents and young children attending child care programs.

National Dissemination Center for Children with Disabilities

http://www.nichcy.org

This web site provides a central information source on disabilities in infants, toddlers, children, and youth.

National Early Childhood Technical Assistance Center

http://www.nectac.org

This web site provides extensive information about disabilities, services for individuals with disabilities, and disability law. Much of the written information is available in multiple languages.

National Resource Center for Health
and Safety in Child Care and Early Education

http://nrc.uchsc.edu

This web site promotes health and safety nationally in out-of-home child care.

U.S. Department of Education

http://www.ed.gov

This web site has extensive information about the No Child Left Behind Act of 2001 (PL 107-110), as well as information for students, parents, teachers, and administrators.

WRITTEN MATERIALS AND PUBLIC LAWS

American Academy of Pediatrics. (2002). *National health and safety performance standards: Guidelines for out-of-home child care programs* (2nd ed.). Elk Grove Village, IL: Author.

American Academy of Pediatrics. (2004). *Managing infectious diseases in child care and schools: A quick reference guide.* Elk Grove, IL: Author.

American Academy of Pediatrics. (2005). *Health in child care manual* (4th ed.). Elk Grove, IL: Author.

Americans with Disabilities Act of 1990, PL 101-336, 42 U.S.C. §§ 12101 *et seq.*

Doggett, L., & George, J. (1993). *All kids count.* Arlington, TX: The Arc.

Great Lakes Resource Access Project. (1992–1993). The Americans with Disabilities Act and Head Start: Practical strategies for developing compliance plans. *Quarterly Resource, 7*(1), 1–15.

Individuals with Disabilities Education Improvement Act of 2004, PL 101-446, 20 U.S.C. §§ 1400 *et seq.*

No Child Left Behind Act of 2001, PL 101-189, 10 U.S.C. §§ 113 *et seq.*

U.S. Department of Justice. (1993). *The Americans with Disabilities Act: Title III technical assistance manual with yearly supplements.* Washington, DC: Author.

U.S. Equal Employment Opportunity Commission. (1993). *Americans with Disabilities Act handbook.* Washington, DC: Author.

C

Summary of Child Care–Related Americans with Disabilities Act Complaints and Litigation

Reasonable modifications of policies, procedures, and practices

Case	State/date	Issue/problem	Complaint process	Outcome/implications
Breen v. State of Connecticut, Department of Public Health and Addiction Services	CT/1994	State nursing regulations do not permit child care personnel to render medical procedures; nursing practices act precludes center from performing test Program refuses to perform finger-prick test for diabetes	Parents sue child care program Parents sue state Parents petition Nursing Board of Examiners to change regulations to allow glucose test to be given	Suit settled with agreement that child continues to attend program and has test done at pediatrician's office nearby Dismissed for failure to exhaust administrative remedies Case has gone to administrative remedy; may return to court
Ireland v. Kansas District of the Wesleyan Church	KS/1994	Three-year-old child dismissed because he or she no longer qualifies for infant room but cannot qualify for toddler room since he or she is unable to walk Licensing regulations establish center capacity on age and ability to walk on his or her own	Filed under Section 504 because church operated but receives federal subsidies; initially granted injunction from disenrolling child Remaining question of whether child is "otherwise qualified" for toddler room	Program ceases to receive federal funds Undisclosed money settlement reached
Stuthard v. KinderCare Learning Centers, Inc.	OH/1996	Child needs finger-prick test and is too young to self-administer; denied admission; no licensing barrier; KinderCare argues giving test fundamentally alters nature of service	Suit filed U.S. Department of Justice begins investigation	KinderCare agrees to perform test procedure; can require parents to sign waiver

(continued)

173

Reasonable modifications of policies, procedures, and practices *(continued)*

Case	State/date	Issue/problem	Complaint process	Outcome/implications
U.S. v. Smyrna Playschool, Inc.	GA/1999	Child care center refused to treat child for asthma by administering an inhaler	Complaint filed with U.S. Department of Justice by parents of the child	Cumberland writes nondiscrimination policy; writes authorization for medical treatment; adopts policy for treating children with severe allergies
Alvarez v. Fountainhead, Inc.	CA/1999	Center refused to administer medication to child with asthma	Parent files suit in District Court	Ordered center to modify its "no medications" policy and enroll a child who has asthma and uses an inhaler; must provide training session for staff on asthma and supervision of children who use albuterol inhalers
E.M. v. Town Sports International, Inc. and TSI Wellesley, Inc.	MA/2006	Center denies participation and refuses to monitor blood glucose level and administer insulin	Parent files suit in District Court	Center agrees to admit child to program and assist in monitoring glucose testing and insulin administration Writes policy and procedures for diabetes management

Denying care or accommodations

Case	State/date	Issue/problem	Complaint process	Outcome/implications
U.S. v. Sunshine Child Care Center	WI/1995	Child, age 4, with cerebral palsy requires diapering and assistance removing and putting on leg braces	Parents file suit against child care center	First case to reach settlement by the U.S. Department of Justice
		Center refuses to accommodate needs and initially wants to retain child in classroom for children under 4 with diapering facilities; finally refuses care	U.S. Department of Justice intervenes	Diapering service can be provided in classroom with diapering facilities
				Child must be integrated into age-appropriate classroom
		Mother (Brock) requests removal of some architectural barriers in parking areas and bathrooms		Center required to eliminate any policy that might exclude other children with disabilities from enrollment related to diapering needs
				Center is barred from requiring any additional documents or waivers not otherwise required of any other families whose children received medication while attending the center
				Center required to remove barriers
				Center must reserve and clearly post accessible parking spaces for use only by families whose members have disabilities

(continued)

175

Denying care or accommodations *(continued)*

Case	State/date	Issue/problem	Complaint process	Outcome/implications
(continued)				Center must publish a nondiscrimination policy in local papers and other written materials to advertise and furnish a copy of the policy to all families served by the center
Orr v. KinderCare Learning Centers, Inc.	CA/1995	Group versus one-to-one care 10-year-old child had full-time personal assistant at no cost to KinderCare KinderCare did not want to allow child to attend, argues fundamentally alters group care and is not a reasonable accommodation	Parents sue child care program	Settlement and consent decree ordered KinderCare to allow child to have personal assistant and be in age-appropriate class
Roberts v. KinderCare Learning Centers, Inc.	MN/1995, 1996	Parents say that acceptance only when accompanied by an aide was failure to reasonably accommodate their child KinderCare says it is group care and one-to-one interaction would fundamentally alter the nature of the service	Parents file suit	U.S. District Court, Minnesota, rules in favor of KinderCare, 1995 Upheld in 8th Circuit District Court of Appeals, 1996

Case	State/Year	Facts	Action	Outcome
J.H. v. ABC Care, Inc.	MD/1996	Plaintiff alleges he has a disability and that defendant wrongfully expelled him from and later refused to readmit him into its after-school child care program	Parents file suit	Summary judgment in favor of defendant No merit to complaint Child not diagnosed until after expelled
Land v. Baptist Medical Center	AR/1999	Parent contends that child's allergy qualifies her as an individual with a disability and that center dismissed her so it would not have to accommodate her disability	Parents file suit	Summary judgment decides in favor of Baptist and dismisses case filed on ADA and ACRA (Arkansas Civil Rights Act) Indicates child does not have a disability Confirms summary judgment of District Court
Burriola v. Greater Toledo YMCA	OH/2001	Child being terminated from child care program Child had been enrolled for 20 months with no mention of termination Mother wants appropriate modifications	Mother files suit	Mother entitled to preliminary injunction against child's termination from child care program Court orders program to take advantage of free training offered by special education program, to make reasonable modifications, and to reinstate child

(continued)

Denying care or accommodations *(continued)*

Case	State/date	Issue/problem	Complaint process	Outcome/implications
U.S. v. Rieck Avenue Country Day School, Inc.	NJ/2004	Child with epilepsy and cerebral palsy refused admission in summer program	Parent initiates complaint	School must admit children with disabilities and adopt a nondiscrimination policy
U.S. v. Joetta Roberts	VA/2003	Wee Care Nursery refuses to continue to serve child of mother who has hepatitis C	Parents file complaint with U.S. Department of Justice	Owner agrees to admit child and attend a training program about ADA obligations of child care providers and adopt a nondiscrimination policy

Eligibility/admissions criteria

Case	State/date	Issue/problem	Complaint process	Outcome/implications
Morrell v. Mexican American Opportunity Foundation	CA/1994	Child's mother dies of AIDS Center refuses to care for child unless tested for AIDS	Suit filed on behalf of child	Settled in favor of child Children cannot be denied care on the basis of their HIV status or status of someone close to them Child care programs are prohibited from requiring testing and/or disclosure of HIV status of children under their care (or those applying for admission) or of anyone closely associated with the children
U.S. v. ABC Nursery Inc. *U.S. v. Happy Time Day Care Center* *U.S. v. Kiddie Ranch*	WI/1997	Centers refuse to admit child who tested HIV positive Centers have criteria that screens out children with disabilities Failure to make reasonable modifications Not afford child opportunity to benefit from services—discrimination	First suit filed by U.S. Department of Justice Suit filed on behalf of guardian and child	Motion of defendants is denied because United States has established that there is a genuine dispute whether child is disabled within the meaning of the ADA Defendants agree that child is disabled under the ADA and agree to hold informational conference on ADA and HIV

(continued)

179

Eligibility/admissions criteria *(continued)*

Case	State/date	Issue/problem	Complaint process	Outcome/implications
U.S. v. Peggy's Child Care	TX/2003	Center refuses to admit 4-year-old child with Down syndrome who needed diapering	Parent files complaint with U.S. Department of Justice	Center agrees to modify its policy to admit children over 3 who are not toilet trained if their need for diapering is due to a disability and provide training on ADA to its employees

Auxiliary aids and services

Case	State/date	Issue/problem	Complaint process	Outcome/implications
U.S. v. Extended Love Child Development	WI/2004	Child with hearing impairment is refused sign language interpreter for communication-intensive activities	Parent files complaint on behalf of child	Center agrees to provide qualified sign language interpreter and auxiliary aids and services when needed to ensure effective communication with children and parents who are deaf or hard of hearing. Agrees to provide staff training

D

Play Areas/
Accessibility Checklist

Play Areas/Accessibility Checklist

Item	Yes	No	Comments
Route of travel and access to equipment			
Path of access—60" wide			
Hard, resilient surface			
Slope no greater than 1:16 (or 1' in height for every 16' in length) maximum; 1:20 minimum (or 1' in height for every 20' in length)			
Transfer points			
Grab bars			
Transfer platform: 11'–14' for children under 5; 12'–17' for children 5–12; platform surface: 2' x 14'			
Parking space (30' x 40') outside of fall zone			
Surface			
Shock-absorbing surface under equipment more than 20" off the ground			
Rest areas			
Close proximity to play equipment			
Description and comments:			

Index

Tables, figures, and footnotes are indicated by *t*, *f*, and *n*, respectively.